Endorsements

"Dave McQuoid is the real deal! By real I don't mean flawless, I mean genuine. When he shares with us in this book his journey with God, and with the grace of God, it has the ring of that which is "real" It is a story that is laced with love, gratitude, and struggle, joy and disappointment, hope and forgiveness, God and the grace of God…and it's genuine. Initially intended to be a gift to his children, and his children's children, Dave's story will now be a gift to us all—reminding us that the grace of God is amazing—it really is amazing grace."

—DAVID JOHNSON
Senior Pastor, Church of the Open Door
Maple Grove, MN

"Dr. David McQuoid has done a phenomenal job of communicating his journey of understanding God's great grace. To know Dr. David is to love him. He is an honest and humble man of integrity whose love for God, family, and life is inspiring. He is the grandpa that everyone wishes they had. His heart is to see the body walk in wholeness in the inner parts of our being. He communicates the heart of a grandpa to see his legacy of love and grace live on in the lives of his family and others. This book will help others become free from self-doubt, discouragement, and even become a grandparent of vision and dreams. Yes, the best is yet to come as you dream big with God."

PASTOR VIVIAN STRONG KLEBS
Pastor of Evangelism, Miracles in the Market Place International
Outreach Director, Urban Mission Training Program

"I've known Dave McQuoid for more than 20 years I have watched him follow Jesus with humility, integrity, and grace. He is a man who has been wounded, broken, and faced with his own brokenness. But the light of Christ has shone in his heart and he has seen the grace and love of God in the eyes of Jesus. Dave has chosen to get up; he has chosen to follow after his Master and Lover of his soul. I wholeheartedly recommend his new book, his story, his response to the amazing grace and love of God through Jesus Christ!"

—Bob McKenna
Care Pastor, Church of the Open Door

"Wow! What a great read! *JUST DAVE, JUST PAPA: Encountering the God of Grace Through the Joys and Challenges of Life* is a very inspiring story of the movements of God that take place over three generations in the McQuoid family. Once I started reading this book, I could not put it down! The transparency and honesty in which Dave McQuoid communicates is compelling. It brought me to tears many times. I encourage you to read Dave's story. The depths of his wisdom are sure to help guide you through many of life's storms and lessons."

—Craig Nelson
Founder of Miracles in the Marketplace International
and The School of Miracles & Ministry

"Whimsically entertaining and truly redemptive—Dave's style of writing grabs and holds the attention of the reader. Dave opens wide the window of his soul and graciously invites us to experience the joys and challenges of his life. Talk about real! Through his autobiography, Doctor Dave gives a treasured gift by which to live. He exemplifies genuineness from the first page to the last. The intimate details of his life's journey range from his mischievousness as a child to God's work of healing and restoration in later life. Enjoy this read of a life well lived!"

—Dave Nelson
Lay pastor of men's ministry, friend, and fellow sojourner

"Intending to write an autobiography for his grandkids, Dave ultimately wrote a wonderful guide book for other grandpas and dads. Written with frank honesty, vulnerability, and integrity, Dave demonstrates his creativity in relating to grandkids and families. As a leader myself working with fathers, I see Dave as a role model and mentor to fathers and grandfathers."

—TIM OLSON
Life coach, pastor, educator, and author

"With a splendid mix of nostalgia, humor, honesty, and spiritual insights, David McQuoid takes you on an inspiring journey through his life. He tells his stories with simplicity and remarkable transparency. You'll read of small-town hijinks in his youth as well as the later struggles and growth toward joy and peace in Christ. This is a memoir of great authenticity—open sharing of faults, shortcomings, and true spiritual breakthroughs of a godly man I know and admire. I highly recommend this book, particularly if you are looking for hope and encouragement. It's a refreshing reminder that God transforms us through all of life's ups and downs."

—QUINTIN STIEFF
Lead pastor, Valley Church
West Des Moines, Iowa

ALUMNI Dr David W McQuoid
2368 W 148th St S Trlr 23
Mitchellville IA 50169-8508

Let me know how you
liked the book if you wish -

Just Dave
Just Papa

Encountering the God of Grace
Through the Joys and Challenges of Life

DAVID W. MCQUOID

Just Dave, Just Papa
Encountering the God of Grace Through the Joys and Challenges of Life

Book cover design: Yvonne Parks, Pear Creative
Interior Typeset: Katherine Lloyd, The DESK

This book is dedicated to our precious grandchildren who have given to their Nona and me barrels of fun, abundant joy, and blessings beyond expectations. This includes all future generations as well.

Christopher, Isabel, Gabriella;
Jacob, Elijah, Luke, Nathaniel;
Derek, Brennan, Ryley; Cody, Zachary;
Rachel, Josiah, Grace, Benjamin

Contents

Introduction

The idea of writing a book was far from my mind most of my life. Beginning in 2004 I started writing short stories about life as a preacher's kid. My older brother and I had several escapades, most noted being the smoking of corncob pipes unbeknownst to our parents. There were a couple of fires that occurred for which no one had an explanation. I noted I enjoyed writing and some family members urged me to write a book.

As grandkids increased I realized they knew very little about my life and the spiritual journey I was on. I began to wonder if I could write a book. I took some classes on writing memoirs that made me feel I should try.

By 2011 my passion to leave a legacy for them and the future generation was very strong. I sensed God was in this, and He orchestrated people and events to help me. I also was very much aware of His presence each time I sat down to write. As I neared the end of writing this book, I realized it was for readers beyond my family as well.

Welcome to my story.

⇥ 1 ⇤

Life Begins

My birth into a Baptist pastor's home had its unique challenges and blessings. Some of my experiences are best told with stories.

Everything began several years before I was born when Dad and Mom laid eyes on each other while attending the Methodist Church at Crosby, Minnesota, in the early 1920s. Mom was an elementary school teacher in the town while Dad worked in an open-pit mine just to the north of Crosby. Sometime after 1925, Dad moved to Minneapolis and got a job with the White Castle Corporation. Mom had to follow her heartthrob, so she found a job teaching in Minneapolis. Their relationship deepened until Dad asked the all-important question. Mom said, "Yes!" and they were married December 26, 1928.

Pastor Dowler, of the Crosby Church, who married them, saw something in my father that impressed him. Thinking Dad would do well in the pastorate, Pastor Dowler encouraged him to pursue that ministry. Dad's initial reaction was, "I'm not cut out to be a preacher." However, the seeds had been planted and soon germinated.

As Dad and Mom prayed about this together, Dad felt led to enter Northwestern Bible and Missionary School, located at First Baptist Church in downtown Minneapolis, where he started their three-year course in the fall of 1929.

Dad enjoyed studying the Bible and was challenged by all the classes he took. He was especially impressed with the founder and first president of Northwestern, Dr. William B. Riley. Because Dr. Riley was also the pastor of the First Baptist Church, Dad was drawn to align himself with that denomination.

Dad's pastoral ministry started when he was still in school. After hearing him preach, the Union Church of Big Lake, Minnesota, called him as a student pastor in the fall of 1931. Following his graduation in June 1932, he and Mom moved to Big Lake, where Dad became their resident pastor.

This started Dad's fifty-seven-year journey of ministry, which included fourteen pastorates and twenty-one churches. He and Mom always sensed a clear direction from God for each place he served, even though his first five positions involved different denominations.

Following his first pastorate at Union Church, Dad felt called to serve three Presbyterian churches in Wisconsin, located at Bennett, Hawthorne and Lake Nebagamon. So my parents moved to Lake Nebagamon in December 1934.

During his years of ministry, Dad and Mom saw God work in many different ways and with varying results, but all for His glory. Finances were always tight but sufficient, as God always provided. Sometimes their needs were met in rather unusual ways as demonstrated by the following story.

Three Bats and Prayer

Several years ago I had a desire to visit my birthplace at Lake Nebagamon, Wisconsin. I asked Dad if he would join me and answer questions I had about my start in life. He was glad to comply, so in the fall of 1979, we made that visit. We found the home in which I was born, and the people living there were very kind, inviting us in to look around. After Dad showed me the downstairs room where I'd been born, we made our way up a narrow stairway to the second floor. As he stood on the landing, Dad pointed to a small square entrance to the attic overhead and told me this story.

Dad and Mom had moved to Lake Nebagamon in 1936, where he became the pastor of three small churches in the area. At the time, they had one baby, Bill, born in 1934, at Big Lake, Minnesota, and Mom was eight months pregnant with me. When they moved to their new location, they bought a crib for Bill but it had no mattress. Since Mom and Dad had shopped without success, Mom began praying daily that they would find the correct size mattress.

In the meantime, Dad had invited Dr. Vallentyne, a well-known preacher, to speak for a week in August at special services he had planned for his churches. Dr. Vallentyne accepted the invitation, agreeing to stay in my parents' home during this time. So Dad began making preparations.

In the middle of the night a week or so before the speaker came, my parents, especially Mom, had the bejeebers scared out of them when a bat flew into their bedroom. (My sister, Jeannie, had a similar experience twenty-five to thirty years later and I imagine Mom and Jeannie's reactions were probably very similar.)

Mom let out a bloodcurdling scream as she pulled the covers over her head. Then she screamed, "Frank, wake up! Something is flying around our bedroom." She followed that with a punch to his ribs.

As he slowly came to and began fumbling for the lamp switch, Dad knocked his eyeglasses on the floor. Once he got the light on and retrieved his glasses, he could see the bat. Dad quickly moved to the bedroom closet, muttering to himself, "Where the heck did that thing come from?" Finding a broom in the closet, Dad knocked the bat into a wall with one mighty swing, where it came crashing to the floor. Dad stomped on it to make sure it would never fly again. With a sigh of relief he said, "It's okay, Mima, you can come out now." (Mima was Dad's pet name for Mom.)

As Mom gradually came out from under the covers, she said tenderly, "My hero. I thank you."

Dad shrugged his shoulders and said, "How did that bat get into the house?" The next morning, he looked carefully for an entry point but couldn't fine one.

Two nights later, the whole scenario repeated itself, except Mom had a lot of tears along with her screaming. Dad's trusty broom brought this bat down too but, with real consternation, he mumbled the same question to himself.

The next morning, in spite of diligently looking under the eaves and every other conceivable place, no portal of entry was found. They were both feeling a lot of anxiety about this since they surely didn't want bats flying around their house, especially while Dr. Vallentyne stayed with them.

A day or two before the speaker arrived, the bat episode happened a third time. My parents slept little the rest of the night, while their prayers for wisdom and direction in this circumstance went to a new level.

The next morning, a light bulb went on in Dad's head. "The attic! I've got to check the attic! Why didn't I think of that before?" He got a stepladder and squeezed through the second floor entrance. He carefully crawled all over but found no entry point for bats. The attic was completely empty except for a lot of dust and one item over in a corner. What do you imagine he found? A crib mattress, which fit the crib perfectly.

Can you guess what other truly amazing thing happened? Never again did any bats appear in their house.

So did God send three bats to tell my parents, "The answer to your prayer is in the attic"? What do you think?

The Family Grows

- Josephine Miriam—born May 29, 1933, at eight months, in a hospital in Minneapolis, Minnesota,— lived a few hours and passed away.

- William (Bill) Holden—born at Big Lake, Minnesota, on July 18, 1934.

- David (Dave) Wentworth—born at Lake Nebagamon, Wisconsin, on September 13, 1936.

- Jeannette (Jeannie) Miriam—born at Lake Nebagamon, Wisconsin, on October 25, 1938.

Dad gave us childhood nicknames that lasted until we were about ten years old. Bill was Tyke, I was Tad, and Jeannie was Tess.

Some of My Baby Book Entries

- November 28, 1936: *"Tyke feeds brother Tad a doorknob screw."*

- December 14, 1937: *"Claps for his brother Tyke every time he says his Christmas piece."*

- April 1, 1938: *"Punished Tyke yesterday by putting him in a corner—scolded Tad today and he voluntarily went into a corner."*

- May 1, 1938: *"Daddy shoveled sand, didn't see Tad nearby and cut his nose with a shovel."* (Author's comment: this is my earliest memory.)

- July 14, 1938: *"Tad's a 'mifitchy' boy— runs away every chance he gets."*

- December 25, 1938: *"Daddy and Mommy gave him a 'ride-'em-choo-choo' but it failed to satisfy—he wanted a wagon like Tyke's."*

After four and a half years of serving the three churches in and around Lake Nebagamon, Dad felt his ministry was coming to an end. He heard that two Bible churches in Sandstone and Rutledge,

Minnesota, were looking for a pastor. Dad contacted them and they asked him to candidate (apply for the job). Feeling Dad was a good man for them, they extended a call, which he happily accepted. So the family moved to Sandstone the first part of May 1939, where one of our many escapades took place.

→ 2 →

Escapades and Frequent Moves; Part of Growing Up

Dad and Mom felt led to move rather frequently during his years of ministry. From the time we moved from Lake Nebagamon to the time I graduated from high school, there were many joys and challenges. Stories and pictures help fill in some of these experiences.

The next five pastorates were unique, challenging, and full of life. On Dad's fourth pastorate he was finally called to a Baptist church. Serving in that denomination was Dad's greatest desire.

I grew physically, mentally, and spiritually, as did my brother and sister. Of course, there were a few escapades along the way.

Sandstone, Minnesota, 5/7/1939—8/17/1941
(Rutledge)

Arrival and settling in

Our family arrived in Sandstone, May 1939. I found a short article in Dad's diary from the *Pine County Courier* newspaper in Sandstone, concerning our arrival. The opening sentence stated, "Rev. Frank McQuoid has received the unanimous call from the Sandstone Bible Church and will begin his new duties next

Sunday." There followed a brief history of his schooling and previous places of ministry. The article closed by saying, "He comes well recommended. The community welcomes him and his family to their new field."

After getting unpacked and settled in the parsonage, Dad began visiting with the members of both churches so he could get to know them. He also planted a garden, which provided many good veggies for the family.

The next spring one of our adventures took place.

Fire in the field

April 13, 1940, was a day forever etched in Bill's and my memories. It started as a cool, spring day. Dad enjoyed writing brief weather reports in his diary and on this day he recorded, "*a high of 34° and a low of 24°.*" We were living in the parsonage of the Sandstone Bible Church and I was just over three, Bill was five and a half, and Jeannie was one and a half.

When I was older I found in Dad's diary where he added his sons' nicknames, calling us Alibi Tyke and Slowpoke Tad. If he had added to Jeannie's nickname it might have been Terrific Tess.

Bill told me recently, as we were recalling the events of that day, how he had loved to play with matches, intrigued with which things would burn or not. There had been a metal holder, with a large box of stick matches, mounted on the wall of the kitchen. A small, trough-like projection extended from the bottom of the holder. When a box of matches was partially opened and slid in from the top, several matches dropped to the trough for easy retrieval. Bill found he could easily remove three or four matches at a time and more would take their place. Therefore, our parents never noticed any matches missing.

On this pleasant, dry, spring Saturday, Dad entered "*S. W. B.*" (southwest breeze) in his diary. He also wrote that he had a short errand to run in Hinckley and, for some important unrecorded reason, Mom went with him. They took Jeannie as well. Since Dad expected to be gone for only a short time, he probably thought he could trust his "mature" sons to stay close to home alone, and to keep out of trouble.

As their car pulled away, I looked at Bill and began to shake with excitement. I heard Bill mutter to himself, "I wonder what new thing I can find to see if it will burn. I wonder if the house would burn. No, better not try that." As I stood waiting for him to decide where or what he would touch a burning match to, I could see him looking across the road at a small open field, owned by our neighbors, Mr. and Mrs. Koland. Bill turned to me and said, "Let's see if we can make a small bonfire in that field."

Bill slipped into the house and took five matches. I think he liked the number five because of the Old Testament story of David picking up five smooth stones before he faced Goliath. We gathered some dry leaves and grass into a small pile in the middle of the field. Bill struck the first match on a nearby rock. He didn't need the other four because, as he touched the burning match to the leaves, there seemed to be, according to our small eyes, an explosion of flames. That southwest breeze did its thing and the flames took off. We stood petrified wondering if the whole world would burn up.

Fortunately, Mr. Koland saw the fire and came running with a gunny sack and a bucket of water. He was able to extinguish the fire by himself as the two of us tore for home, in tears over the results of our experiment.

Soon our parents arrived home and found us both crying and shaking like the leaves we'd just burned. They asked us what happened, and Bill, true to his nickname, replied, "I was standing on a rock and there were some matches under my foot. I slipped and a match caught the leaves on fire."

The facts, as stated in Dad's diary, were: "*Tyke sets a fire back of A. Koland's. Tad squeals.*" The usual discipline for such serious misbehavior in our home was a spanking, so I probably squealed to try and save my hide. That didn't happen this time since the scare we had was almost punishment enough. However, Bill was confined to his room for a half day as Dad entered: *"Tyke stays in his room one half day as penalty for Sat. aft."*

Interestingly, the penalty didn't apply until two days after the episode. I presume with Saturday baths, et cetera, it was too late in the day. And since Sunday was "the Lord's day," Dad probably felt it was inappropriate to punish on that day. In fact, Dad recorded on Sunday afternoon: *"I kicked Tyke's football for him in the aft. In eve. Tad said, 'You kicked the ball way up to Jesus' house.' 'Where is that?' 'Way up in Heaven.' 'What is Jesus doing up there?' 'He isth wathing dithes.'"* (I had a lisp at that age.)

Thus ended the experiments on what would burn. I'm quite sure of one thing, however, the matches were relocated in a much higher and safer place.

A difficult ending

Dad and Mom enjoyed the community of believers in both churches he pastored, and they seemed to appreciate his preaching. However, Dad was unaware of a small group within the Sandstone church, which for unknown reasons, became dissatisfied with him.

The church constitution required that the pastor be voted on each year and it only took one third of the members casting a negative ballot to oust him. In the evening, after the annual meeting during his second year in April 1941, he made this diary entry: *"Church voted us out, 40 - 22."*

In the summer of 1991, I revisited Sandstone to take pictures of where I once lived. I visited with Russ and Abby Soderquist, dear friends of my parents, who were members of the same Bible church when we were there. Russ explained that he and his wife were in the kitchen cleaning during the annual meeting, having no clue what was happening. Dad lost by one vote. They were heartsick because they loved him, his family, and his preaching. Russ told me that after the vote, "Dad graciously asked what was wrong, but no one answered." Later someone said they voted against him, "just to keep him on his toes."

Dad was not one to express his emotions but he wrote in his diary the next evening, *"A day of nothing but headaches and soul illness."* On the third day he entered, *"Tried to study but not much accomplished."* The following evening was different as he wrote, *"Studied most of the day. God blesses through Psalm 66."*

The next day was Sunday and Dad was in the pulpit. In the evening he entered this statement, *"God gave me grace and peace!"*

Dad continued ministering at the Sandstone church for three months. His entry on that last day was, *"God gives grace."* His last service at the Rutledge church was two weeks later.

Searching for the next pastorate

This was not an easy task as Dad diligently and prayerfully looked for another place of service. A week after the vote he wrote, *"Corresponding with Iowa churches."* Mid-May, Dad took a train to Kansas City to attend a conference, hoping to find some leads. In August, Dad got a manual job with REA for a week, digging holes and putting in posts, to help put food on the table. Later on, Dad went to a Bible conference west of Minneapolis at Medicine Lake, but still found no possible openings.

The first part of September, Dad returned to the Twin Cities and Northwestern Bible School to have a *"conference with Drs. Moyer and Riley."* They discussed the possibility of Dad joining the United Brethren denomination. That resulted in Dad attending their annual conference in Bloomington, Illinois, the next week where he was interviewed by the leaders and approved.

On the last day of the conference, Dad learned they were sending him to Allendale, Illinois, where he would pastor four small UB churches. His diary entry that evening stated, *"Praise the Lord.*

Wire Mima Psalm 126:3" That verse (KJV) says, *"The Lord has done great things for us; we are glad."*

Allendale, Illinois, 9/14/1941—8/20/1944
(Adams Corner, Patton, Nye Chapel, and Pleasant Grove were the four small churches under Dad's new pastorate.)

Settling in

Dad hired a trucker to move our possessions while we crawled into our '37 Chevy, pulling a heavily loaded trailer, and headed south. That was the last Friday of September 1941. We spent the day in Minneapolis so Dad could officiate at the marriage of his sister, Eleanor, to Leonard Bagne. *"Very beautiful! A fine service,"* he wrote in his diary.

After three more days of driving, we arrived at our new home. It was a parsonage in the country near Adams Corner, outside of Allendale, Illinois. As we drove onto the dirt driveway, Mom gasped with wonder and shed a few tears. There was a small two-story, beautiful, brick house with a front porch extending the length of the house. It looked like a mansion to her. We were all excited to check it out.

Inside there was a large wood- and coal-burning potbelly stove on one side of the living room. That supplied the heat for the house in the cold winter months. Mom was pleased to see the kitchen had a nice cooking stove that also burned wood or coal. After unpacking she would be ready to prepare the wonderful meals we all loved. The bedrooms were upstairs, which was a good thing since there was no insulation in the house and heat rises. Dad placed bales of straw around the outside of the house in the fall to help keep some of the winter cold out.

The house had a cellar, which always had a pungent, moldy smell, with an outside entrance and stairs leading down to a dirt floor. Shelves on one side held jars for canning, which Dad and Mom did each fall with produce from our garden. On the other side of the cellar was a makeshift half-wall designed to hold coal. There was a metal slide extending up to an outside window at ground level. A truck loaded with coal would back up to that window, open it, and dump a ton or so into the cellar whenever we needed it.

Dad worked hard

Dad started his new pastorate during World War II when there was rationing. He had a salary of $875 per year, which required him to help support his family in other ways.

We became small-scale farmers with a good-sized garden in which the "men" of the house toiled. As kids, our respective ages that first fall, were seven, five, and three, with Tess (Jeannie) in the house helping Mom most of the time.

We also had a large chicken house with twenty-plus chickens that supplied eggs and meat. Then we had Star, a milking cow, Cheop, a female pig for raising and selling piglets, plus Betty, Beauty, and several other goats for milk.

Dad also worked side jobs of various types. He became the caretaker of the Adams Corner church cemetery, which meant Tyke and I were asked to do trimming and some mowing. Dad *"worked on the slab"* as recorded in his diary, which meant employment by the highway department for road work. One year he had a job at the Snap-on Tools factory working the 4 p.m. to 1 a.m. shift on weekdays. Dad purchased a motorcycle, which was cheap transportation to his various jobs.

Star watch and butter

We all had assigned jobs to do. I helped Tyke gather the eggs daily. Tyke also had to be sure the goats were securely tied because if one got loose he had to chase it down.

We had a small barn/garage on the parsonage property for

the farm animals at night and during bad weather. My job was to keep an eye on Star when she was tied up near the garden as she loved to break loose and feed on the garden produce, especially the corn. I had a second job as well. Mom took the rich cream from Star's milk, put it into a two-quart jar and asked me to shake it until it became butter, which I did, sitting on the lawn and watching Star.

One especially hot, sunny day, when I was about five, I was given that double task. I got very tired from shaking the cream, but finally it turned to butter. I was feeling sorry for myself as I trudged into the house half crying and lisped to Mom, "Ith not fair for one boy tho have thwo thobs!"

My parents laughed over that story many times as they told it to others. I didn't think it was very funny.

Starting school

The small country school where I started first grade in the fall of 1942, was for grades one through eight. Mitchell Alcorn, the teacher, was a warm and friendly man. Since I was the only one in first grade, he let me work as hard and fast as I wanted, which resulted in my finishing both first and second grade requirements in my first year. At the time it was thought to be a good thing, but I realized much later that emotionally and athletically I was almost two years behind where I was academically.

Moving again

Dad attended the annual United Brethren conference at Decatur, Illinois, in mid-August 1944. He met with *"the stationing committee."* His diary indicated this committee had the responsibility of relocating pastors to new places of ministry as they felt led. On the last day of the conference, Dad learned he was being sent to Canton, Illinois, to pastor two churches, Shields Chapel and Locust Lane.

This required Dad to sell most of the livestock in preparation for the move. Since the new location was also in the country, he was able to take some of his chickens and goats, especially Beauty and Betty, our favorites.

Canton, Illinois, 9/3/1944—6/24/1945
(Shields Chapel, Locust Lane)

Settling in again

The move was much easier this time in that it was only a 260-mile drive. However, the packing and unpacking was the same laborious process. The parsonage was next to the Shields Chapel church, which, in turn, was kitty-corner across a gravel road from the one-room country school we attended. We arrived near the start of school where I entered fourth grade, Tyke, sixth, and Tess, first.

Beauty and the teacher's car

Dad liked having goats because of their milk and they were fairly low maintenance. He brought five of them from Allendale.

However, we had a star among the group named Beauty, who was very social and loved to show off in front of people. Her favorite act was to jump up onto the roof of a car and dance. This began a short time after church on Sunday mornings. Beauty would do her dance on one car, jump down, go to another car roof and repeat her dance. I don't know if Dad had trimmed her hoofs or not, but no scratches or damage was done to the cars. Tyke always had a rope tied securely around her neck so she couldn't run away. Everyone enjoyed the entertainment, but the kids especially thought it was a hoot.

Dad frequently tied the goats to such a place because of the ample supply of grass for them to enjoy. He knew that Beauty would see us going back to school after lunch and would try to follow us. One school day when the three of us came home for lunch, Tyke got the mischievous idea to loosen the rope that securely tied Beauty to a tree next to a ditch.

Shortly after school started for the afternoon, the teacher began screaming at the top of her lungs, "There's a goat dancing on my car roof!" She had recently purchased the car.

Tyke tore out of the room, grabbed the rope tied to Beauty's neck, and got her down. But Beauty, being the social butterfly that she was, headed for the open door to the school, jerked her rope out of Tyke's hand, and proceeded to dance from one desktop to another. This thrilled the students and they laughed and cheered her on. Since the teacher was beside herself with consternation, Tyke quickly grabbed Beauty's rope, took her back to the tree, and securely tied her to it.

After school the teacher had a talk with Dad. We don't know what was said but we're pretty sure it wasn't about his sermon the previous Sunday. All he said to us was, "I can't figure out how that goat got loose."

Who broke the school window?

Sometime during the fall, Dad decided to teach us how to make and use slingshots. I guess he saw us throwing rocks at trees and cans, which gave him the idea. We were excited to learn. He taught us to be very careful wherever we were shooting the slingshot, so we practiced on cans and various other objects. We actually got pretty good at hitting an object if it was big enough, like a tree.

Early summer of the following year after school was out, Tyke and I were walking along the gravel road next to the school. We were practicing our skill with the slingshots when we noticed a turtledove sitting on an overhead electric wire. Without looking at what was on the other side I took aim and let a stone fly. I just missed the bird, but the stone continued on its high-arcing path and then began to descend. I suddenly realized it was heading right for the school, and crack! it went right through a window. We quickly stuffed our slingshots into our respective pockets and walked along as if nothing had happened.

A couple of days later a school board member stopped by our house and asked Dad, in our presence, "Have you seen anyone shooting a gun around here lately?"

Dad's response was in the negative, so the man redirected the question to us.

We looked at each other, then at the board member, and Tyke said, "No, we haven't seen any gunfire around here." The board member walked away scratching his head.

Later, Tyke and I went over to the school, looked into the window with the hole in it and saw the stone lying on the floor with broken glass particles around it. We puzzled over why the board member had never looked through the window to the floor. He wasn't a very good detective.

I felt like I had dodged a bullet!

Dad's heart's desire fulfilled

Though Dad enjoyed the ministry he had at the United Brethren Churches of Shields Chapel and Locust Lane, his longing still was to be in a Baptist church, which his diary indicated. In his entry on April 3, 1945, he wrote briefly about other things, but he ended with two words: *"Wrote Baptist."* That meant he wrote to someone who knew of possible openings in Baptist churches in the upper Midwest. The next entry May 16, 1945, showed he'd found what he was looking for: *"Mima and I plan on candidating at El Salem Baptist on Sunday,"* resulting in a call for that church. He resigned from the above two churches and we moved to the new place of ministry near Nye, Wisconsin, the first part of July.

Ubet, Wisconsin, 7/8/1945—6/5/1949

A new location

The usual packing and loading of the moving van, trailer, and car was followed with unloading at the other end, where a welcoming party of church people helped us unload and unpack. Dad and Mom were so happy to finally be ministering in a Baptist church.

The church and parsonage were located in the country, five miles east of Dresser, Wisconsin, with farmland all around. There were woods to the north and west of us that provided excellent rabbit and squirrel hunting. An intersection a half-mile to the west of the church was the "metropolis" known as Ubet, with a sign: Population four. It had a grocery store owned by the Routy family and an auto repair garage belonging to the Eastman's.

The farms were usually one-fourth to one-half mile apart and we soon made friends with the neighborhood kids. Mr. Eastman had made a basketball court in his garage so, when he was not working on a car, Bill and I could play two on two against Allen Eastman and his cousin, Jim Routy. They were both Bill's age, around ten, when we first moved there. I think they usually beat us.

Ubet school

A half-mile south of Ubet was the Ubet school, a brick, one-room building that opened in 1930. There I went to fifth and sixth grade before the school closed in the spring of 1947. There were ten to twelve students, grades one through eight in that school, with only one teacher. We rode our bikes to school most of the time, weather permitting, or walked in the wintertime.

I remember telling my kids, many years later, how I used to walk in deep snow three or four miles to school. So one fall day, I decided to take my family for a ride from our home in Golden Valley, Minnesota, to Ubet, Wisconsin, about sixty miles away. I wanted to show them where I'd lived and gone to school for two years of my life. You can imagine my chagrin and my family's raucous laughter when the distance from my boyhood home to the school was barely a mile.

For some reason, the teacher and the students at the Ubet school were like oil and water—they didn't mix. On occasion, someone would throw a wad of paper at the teacher when she was writing on the blackboard with her back toward us. But there seemed to be a special animosity between my brother and the teacher.

One day she passed out a sheet of paper to each student. In an attempt to smooth the rough waters between herself and the students, the teacher asked each student to write down what they did not like about her. As some students began writing, Bill raised his hand. When the teacher called on him he asked, "May I have a second sheet?" Needless to say, that did not improve the feelings between the two.

On one occasion, at a community meeting, the teacher suggested a picnic as a get-together. There was a favorable response to the idea until the date was set for a Sunday afternoon. Dad had a strong religious belief that such an activity should not take place on "the Lord's day." He spoke against the idea and as Bill said, "He took on the whole community." The debate became heated and the teacher canceled the picnic, and all three of us kids became, in Bill's words, "dead meat."

The next day as we were riding our bikes home from school, we were hijacked at the Ubet intersection by the "school bullies," where they knocked us off our bikes, and threw them into a deep, nearby ditch. Such was the joy of being PKs (preacher kids).

Ubet escapades

Living in the country with woods behind our home gave us a lot of squirrels and rabbits to hunt as a food supply. We also had a large garden. Dad gave Bill a single shot Remington rifle and taught him how to shoot it, giving both of us lessons in gun safety. All I had was a Daisy BB gun. When we went hunting, I jumped on a brush pile to scare out a rabbit. Once, a rabbit took off on a dead run and Bill got it with one shot to the head. Wow, what a shot!

Looking back, there was one humorous escapade, though scary

at the time, that had to do with corncob pipes. On the Matson farm, a quarter of a mile away, two guys our ages, Jack and Paul, lived. Their dad smoked Camel cigarettes and on occasion, Paul would secretly help himself to a few. He gave us a couple once but we became so dizzy and sick we didn't want to touch them again.

Paul then showed us how to make corncob pipes so we could smoke corn silk. We took a corncob, shelled of its corn, and cut it about three inches long. Then we drilled out the center, except for the bottom, and a small hole in the side of the cob into which we inserted a hollow reed. Finally, we gathered some dry corn silk, packed it into the cob and lit up. Boy, we felt like big shots as we sat around Paul's barn smoking our pipes.

Then we got the idea to take our pipes to school on the sly and smoke during recess. That only lasted one day before the teacher caught us. She threatened expulsion from school if she ever caught us again. So someone got the idea to store our stash in a pea-vinery shack located across the road from the Ubet grocery store. The local farmers used the scale, housed inside the shack, to weigh their trucks loaded with peas just harvested. The shack was unlocked and had a broken board in the floor that we could easily lift up. There was ample space underneath to tuck in our supplies, safe from the eyes of any farmer using the scale. This became a great place to stop for a smoke on the way home from school. I was ten and Bill, twelve.

One day after our usual "smoke after school," I sat down to practice my piano lesson while Bill did some of his jobs. Meanwhile, back at the pea-vinery shack one of the pipes (I said it was Bill's and he was sure it was mine) used that day, fanned into flames from a breeze blowing through that very porous shack. In a brief amount of time, the entire shack was in flames. I was diligently practicing my lesson when Bill came running into the living room, white as a ghost. He whispered in my ear, "The pea-vinery shack is burning down!"

I gasped, turned white like him, and went to the bathroom. When I came out I tried to finish practicing but it was very hard with my heart pounding like a drum. My music couldn't keep up with my heartbeat.

The community owners of the shack figured some kids had set it on fire or left some smoking equipment still burning but couldn't figure out the culprits. Dad and Mom never had a clue; certainly, their wonderful, upstanding sons would not be involved!

Bill and I laid low for a while, but the incredible "addictive" power of corn silk began to raise its ugly head—we just had to have some more puffs. We not only had to find a new place for our stash, but we had to make new pipes, a trade in which we were becoming masters.

One day while hunting in the woods behind our place, we found a tree near the edge of the forest, still standing, although the inside and bottom were rotted out. That made a wonderful secret place to hide our stuff. So after school, when piano practice and jobs were done, we'd slip away for a walk in the woods, taking our guns so it looked like we were hunting. Boy, we were big stuff!

That fantasy came to a screeching halt a few days later when we heard Dad loudly call for us to get some buckets of water. Mr. Eastland was trying to put out a fire in one of the trees on the edge of his woods. It was a sunny, breezy day with no threat of lightning anywhere in the sky. Dad and Mr. Eastland were completely baffled as to how that tree caught fire. At least the fire burned up all the evidence.

Bill and I figured two narrow escapes were enough. A third time might be a complete strikeout. Our addiction to corn silk was cured—we never touched the stuff again. At least, I haven't, but I can't be so sure about my brother. I think there have been a couple of strange, unexplained fires in his home.

We had many other experiences during the four years we lived there, like the time Bill and I caught over fifty sunfish at a nearby creek after a big rain.

One time, a skunk came through a window and crawled into a hole in our cellar. Dad was able to chloroform it one night without it spraying.

Another time, because of the number of skunks we had around us, Dad warned all the neighboring farmers to keep their dogs inside for twelve hours because he was going to put out some meatballs with strychnine in them. We were dog-sitting for good friends of ours while they were on a trip so we kept their dog, Major, locked up that night. The next day, part of a meatball was missing and Dad couldn't find it. Unfortunately, Major found it, ending his life.

A third time, a skunk got into a small classroom in the church. I, unwisely, tried to shoot it with a slingshot, before the skunk sprayed and took off out of the church. The odor stayed in that room for years.

A close call

On April 23, 1949, when I was twelve, we had one of those gorgeous spring days with the sun shining bright, the birds singing their joyous melodies, and fluffy white clouds drifting lazily overhead. I had completed what jobs Dad or Mom had assigned me and I now had free time to do one of the things I enjoyed most, riding my bike.

I'd ridden my bike many times down that old gravel road past farm after farm. One of my jobs was to ride to a farm three miles away, then bring home three or four gallons of fresh milk right after the farmer milked his cows. It was usually in the evening when I made a milk run and often the stars were coming out. Once a falling star streaked across the sky startling me so much that I went into a ditch, spilling some of the milk.

There was one farm that I *always* pedaled past as fast as I could since the owners had a bulldog. I thought he was the most ferocious animal that ever lived. Frequently he would chase me when

I went by but, because I was flying like the wind, he could never catch me. I could only imagine what my leg would look like if he ever grabbed me.

So on this particular day, I was enjoying my bike with a strong wind at my back. I decided to get my bike up to top speed to see how far I could coast before I came to a full stop. I cranked my single-speed up as fast as I could, then sat back, making myself as big as possible to catch as much wind as I could. Oh, it was so much fun to just coast along letting the wind do the work. Gradually the bike began going slower and slower until it finally stopped. I took a deep breath of satisfaction having thoroughly enjoyed the experience.

Suddenly I became aware of my surroundings and realized, to my complete shock, I was just across the road from where that not-so-friendly animal lived. To my absolute horror, the bulldog was coming down the driveway, full speed ahead with a direct bead on me. I think I was probably ashen white and ready to wet my pants or do something even worse. I was frozen with fear as the dog came out of the driveway and onto the road, by my childish estimation, running at least fifty miles per hour.

The next thing that happened seems frozen in time. Neither the dog nor I was aware of a car coming up behind me. As the bulldog entered the road heading straight toward where I was standing behind my bike with shaking knees, the car struck that ferocious creature with its front left wheel, killing the bulldog instantly, never knowing what hit him.

I gulped, hopped on my bike, and slowly rode away, looking back frequently at my enemy lying dead on the road. My heart pounded like a sledgehammer. I saw the driver of the car stop and inform the owner that he'd just killed his dog. At least I assume that's what happened, not hanging around to ask questions. Although I don't remember, I'm quite sure that as I rode away I was offering up a prayer of gratefulness that my guardian angel was present and doing his job.

Farewell

After four years of ministry at El Salem Baptist, Dad sensed that his ministry was coming to a close. He resigned May 1, 1949, not sure of what was next. He wrote letters to the appropriate people and found there was an opportunity at the First Baptist Church in Lake Benton, Minnesota. He candidated there mid-May and received the call to come six days later. We packed up and moved in June.

Lake Benton, Minnesota, 6/9/1949—5/31/1953

Lake Benton was located in the southwest corner of Minnesota. It had the same name as the nearby seven-mile-long lake adjacent to the town. I'll never forget, as a twelve-year-old, the beautiful, picturesque view of this small town snuggled in a valley as we drove south on highway US 75. The valley was called the Hole-in-the-Mountain on Buffalo Ridge.

Before we started into the valley, Dad turned left on a gravel road to the east and stopped the car where we had a beautiful view of the lake and town. There he prayed a special blessing over the community, the First Baptist Church, and the ministry that he was entering.

The town had a population of just under a thousand, but to me it seemed like such a big place compared to living in the country. The church was located on the southeast corner of the main intersection, next to the business section, with the parsonage just behind the church.

As soon as we got settled into our new home, Bill and I began urging Dad to get our basketball hoop up on the front of our one-car garage. Because we kept bugging him, he finally put it up. We once again enjoyed shooting hoops.

Half a block to the south was a nice park with a softball field.

That was where we played football or baseball. In the winter, the fire department flooded an area for skating.

The school was two blocks east of our home, a large, brick building, perched on a hill that looked pretty awesome to my twelve-year-old eyes. Going there was a totally new experience for my sister, Jeannie, starting sixth grade, and myself, starting ninth grade, as the school had grades one through twelve, along with many extracurricular opportunities. Class sizes ranged from twenty-five to thirty.

It was different for Bill since he had already spent two years at St. Croix Falls High School in Wisconsin. Here he was entering eleventh grade. The real shocker, however, was going from twelve-man football to six. He'd never heard of such a thing as six-man football and was pretty disgusted initially, but he made the adjustment.

Favorite teachers

Mr. H.G. Edwall was our high school principal the four years I was at Lake Benton. He also was my math teacher. I liked his friendliness, along with his concern and willingness to help his students. Mr. Edwall was a great encourager and I felt he took a special interest in me, although he gave that same impression to a lot of his students.

Mr. Tom Rossiaky was my history teacher and head coach in the three main sports of football, basketball, and baseball. He was such a likable guy with a wonderful sense of humor, known for smoking a big pipe any time he wasn't in the classroom. He loved coaching and, even more, the guys who played for him. He also encouraged me, and for some reason, gave me the nickname, McKoodle Cuddle. He'd call me that and then just laugh.

I was touched my senior year when Mr. Rossiaky, in my copy of *The Bobcat*, our year book wrote, "To an excellent student, the best basketball player I have had the pleasure of coaching.

Tom Rossiaky."

Miss Phyllis Umland taught home economics and vocal music. She had a beautiful voice and a sparkling personality that brought out the best in those who sang under her direction. I enjoyed singing with my buddy, Roland, in the Boys Octette and the Senior Choir.

My best buddy

His name was Roland Jordahl, nicknamed George. We hit it off from day one when we volunteered to be on the school patrol together. We also learned to make fudge, although the first batch was so hard and bad we threw it away, including the pan, which Mom wasn't very happy about. But we improved as we worked on it. One day we gave a piece of fudge to Phyllis Umland and she was impressed. She also gave us some tips on how to better our product.

We did a lot of skating together at the rink in the park or down at the lake. George reminded me about the time my dad let me drive the car to the rink a block away for an evening of skating. When we were done, and since home was so close by, I didn't bother to take my skates off to drive. As I entered our garage I couldn't get my foot loose to hit the brake. I plowed into the front of the garage. Dad heard the crash and came running. George said, when Dad realized what I'd done, "He gave you a stern sermon on 'the wrong of driving a car with skates on.'" I think he probably did more than that but I don't remember.

In the winters of our junior and senior years, George and I got the job of shoveling snow from the school sidewalks, which were quite long leading up the hill to the school. We also shoveled the snow from the front of the garage housing the four school buses. George said, "The best part of the job were the giant pancakes your mom made for us early in the morning." They really energized us for the work ahead.

Probably our biggest claim to fame as a duo was that we were the champions of our high school annual badminton doubles tournament. We were champs in both our junior and senior years.

I'm glad to say that our friendship has still stayed strong over the years.

Music

When we were at El Salem, Mom taught each of us to play the piano. But we had to do our daily jobs, including practice, before we could go play. When we moved to Lake Benton we were permitted to switch to another instrument. Bill took up the trumpet, and Jeannie the saxophone, though she continued with the piano. I chose the trombone. Dad drove us to Marshall, Minnesota, for weekly lessons with our respective instruments. We all played in the school band and marching band. We also performed at various church services and youth meetings during our high school years.

Once, Jeannie, on the piano and I, on the trombone, were in a music contest in a nearby town. We won first place and received the grand reward of three dollars.

Sports

Bill and I took part in all the sports available at the school. However, football was his game and basketball mine. I was on the starting five for both my junior and senior years. Our basketball team my senior year was pretty good and we thought we had a chance to make it out of the district tournament into the regional, but lost a nail-biter that ended our dream.

I was honored to be placed on the All-Conference starting five team and then the All-District starting five.

College

Early in my senior year of high school, I began to think about college. I didn't have a clue where I should go or what course of study I should pursue, so I asked Dad if he had any suggestions. His reply was simple, "Why don't you go to the school where Bill is going and take the same classes he is taking?" So what were Bill's plans?

Bill had graduated from Lake Benton High School two years ahead of me. The first year he'd gone to St. Paul Bible Institute and his second year, done various jobs in Minneapolis. Once in a Sunday school weekly magazine, *Power*, Bill read an article about a Wheaton College track coach, Gil Dodds. Another time he read about a Wheaton College football player, and thought that Wheaton might be a good place for him to attend.

Bill stayed at the YMCA in Minneapolis for a period of time in 1952. There he met an older gentleman with whom he enjoyed many conversations. On several occasions this older friend said to him, "Bill, you're a real smart guy. I bet you'd make a good doctor." Bill had no idea where that came from but it planted seeds in his mind.

The result was that we both applied to Wheaton College and were accepted for the fall of 1953. Bill had to take a one-month course at Wheaton summer school to qualify, but we both entered Wheaton as pre-med students. We packed up our earthly belongings in Dad's car and he and Mom drove us to Wheaton on September 10, 1953, where a whole new life began for both of us.

⇥ 3 ⇤

Pursuit of Academia
and My Life's Partner

*An interest in science and math, starting in my high school
years, along with Dad's suggestion, led me to the pre-med
pathway at college and then on to medical school. While
in college I met the dream of my life, who became my life's
partner after my first year of medical school. The final step,
following medical school, was a one-year rotating internship
at an excellent hospital that prepared me for my first practice in family medicine.*

Entering Wheaton College brought a whirlwind of activity and
new experiences.

College Life

Settling in

Once we were settled in our room in one of the men's dormitories, Culp Hall, Bill and I each received a "Big Brother," an
upperclassman who helped guide us through the first weeks of
adjusting to college life. We registered for classes, which included
Math, Chemistry, Chemistry lab, English, Bible, and ROTC
(Reserved Officer Training Corps). Since we both started off as
pre-med students, we took the same classes.

Classes were intense with a lot of homework, a big step up compared to high school days. Yet it was amazing and what a blessing to be in a Christian school where professors would have a short devotional before the start of each class. We had Chapel services every weekday morning, with great speakers. There was an atmosphere of friendliness, peace, and respect that made me very glad to be at this school.

In our first year, Bill went out for football and played on the Bomber (freshman) Squad. I chose basketball and was excited to make the freshman team as well.

Variety of jobs

I had to work to make ends meet and spent many hours in my four years washing pots and pans and cleaning floors in the dining hall. The employment office had lists of jobs people offered in the city of Wheaton, or surrounding communities so I raked a lot of leaves on Saturday or washed windows.

During my senior year I got a night job with the Chicago, Aurora, and Elgin Railroad. I operated one of several towers on the crossings in Wheaton. A buzzer told me of an approaching train so I could lower the gates before and raise them after the train passed. Fortunately, I was able to do a lot of studying between trains.

Once in the wee morning hours, I dozed off while the gates were down for a long train. A policeman had to wake me up in order to raise the gates. That was not a good performance.

Roommates

It was great to have my big brother as my roommate for the first year and a quarter. Bill sustained a concussion playing football in our second year at college, and he had to drop out of school. I really missed him.

Don Anderson from Colorado, had become a good friend of mine and became my next roommate. He was a year ahead of me at Wheaton, and was quite a whistler. Once he came home with me to Luverne, Minnesota. Dad heard him whistle and liked what he heard, so in one of the weekend church services he asked Don to whistle one of the hymns. As I recall, he did whistle it and was great.

Don met his life's partner, Cara Van Boven, at Wheaton. And in my senior year I was privileged to be best man in their wedding.

Phil Gegner became my roommate my senior year. We had a blast together because he had a car. Phil was an art major and got me to pose in a swimsuit for one of his art classes. He also did a beautiful oil painting of Anna, which became a surprise gift to me at our Wheaton engagement party. That painting still hangs in our home.

Christian service

A part of being a student at Wheaton College was the challenge of involvement in a ministry of some kind. It wasn't required, but there were so many different opportunities that it was easy to find one you liked.

My freshman year, I joined a group that went into Skid Row in downtown Chicago on Sundays. That was a challenging and heart-wrenching experience. We wanted to share the good news of the gospel to the addicted down-and-outers. There were some who were touched and had their lives changed.

Don Anderson introduced me to the "colored Sunday school," as they were called at that time. There were several groups of Wheaton students involved in this ministry. Don was also the leader of a group known as Joy Sunday school.

Each Sunday we bypassed the best meal of the week in the dining hall for a bagged lunch, boarded a bus, and drove into Southside Chicago to a designated area. We had teams of two, a guy and a gal, known as route partners. Each team had a designated circuit where we went door-to-door, inviting children to come to Sunday school in the afternoon. We engaged the adults in conversation and invited them to an adult class as well.

At noon our groups met at the apartment of Mrs. Hicks, a lovely Christian lady with five kids. She had opened her place for us to meet, eat our lunch, and pray together. Later in the afternoon each team retraced their route and brought all the kids and adults who were interested to a building where the Sunday school was held. Following Sunday school, teams took the kids back to their respective apartments. Discussion in the bus ride home often revolved around what God had done in the lives of the people we had touched that day.

When Don graduated from Wheaton, he passed the leadership baton to me to lead Joy Sunday school in my senior year. It was a privilege and honor to accept.

Bill's Dream Comes True

Motorcycle Maniacs

What does a young man of nineteen, in his first year of college, do with five hundred dollars that's burning a hole in his pocket? Does he pay school bills? Of course not! Does he notice his younger brother's dire need of financial help and offer to share some of it with him? No way! So what does he do? He goes out and buys a motorcycle. Such was the scenario that transpired with my older, mature, wise brother at Wheaton College the first part of June 1954.

Bill and I got summer jobs at Paulson's Dehydrating Plant in Luverne, Minnesota, our new home. While on the job, Bill had an accident, breaking both arms, and had to spend half the summer of 1953 with his arms in casts. However, he'd healed well by the time we entered Wheaton as freshmen and roommates. Bill received a final settlement of one thousand dollars from Workers Compensation Insurance and managed to spend half of it on various and sundry needs. But he still had five hundred bucks left in his checking account that he kept thinking about.

Although Bill had no experience in riding a motorcycle, it had always been his dream to own one. Dad had owned a small Indian cycle ten years prior during the gas rationing of the World War II years. Maybe that was when the motorcycle bug bit Bill.

Bill had a half-day break during exam week the first part of June. So he hopped on the Aurora-Elgin commuter train that went the thirty miles into Chicago, Illinois. He found a large motorcycle dealership, strolled into the store with a swagger, and announced to the dealer: "I have five hundred dollars and not a penny more. I want to buy a bike."

The dealer, being duly impressed with the straightforwardness and maturity of this young man standing before him replied, "I'm sure we can fix you up. Have you ever ridden a motorcycle before?"

Bill gave him an indignant look and said, "Of course I have."

The two of them began looking over the large number of bikes available. Bill decided on a Harley-Davidson. It was a 1948 Pan head model with a 74 cubic inch engine known as a "Harley 74." The motorcycle had an expired license plate, but the dealer, learning that Bill was heading to Minnesota, told him to cut out a piece of cardboard, write "licensed applied for" on it, and secure it to the license plate holder. He could then get a license when he got home. That sounded good to Bill so he forked over the money, jumped on his Harley, and drove off, nearly clipping a few cars and road signs until he got the hang of riding his new bike.

Bill arrived safely back in Wheaton where we packed for our exciting trip home the next day. I had an exam that day that lasted until 3:30 p.m., and as it was getting late, we wanted to hit the open road. Our original plan was to drive the five hundred miles straight through to Luverne, Minnesota.

On a beautiful, sunny day, late afternoon on June 10, 1954, we drove out of Wheaton, full of excitement and really cocky about our anticipated trip. As we were driving off campus heading north, unbeknownst to us, the Wheaton College wrestling coach and assistant football coach, Mr. George Olson, stood on a corner watching us drive by.

Three months later, when Bill returned to school ready for football practice, Mr. Olson told Bill he'd had a premonition of danger and been concerned as he saw us driving out of town. He'd thought, "Those McQuoid boys are crazy. They don't know what they're doing," but stood on the corner and prayed for our safety as we drove away.

Looking back now, I know Mr. Olson was right. Little did we know the importance of his prayers as we left Wheaton.

I remember the thrill I felt as we drove along with the wind blowing through our hair. Of course, we weren't wearing helmets—that just wasn't macho. Besides, I knew we would be okay because my older brother was driving and, by now, appeared to be a seasoned driver. I do remember, however, as the hours went by that my rear end sure got sore and my legs became stiff from sitting still, unable to wiggle even a little bit. We stopped ever so briefly now and then to stretch, but our goal was to get home in twelve to fourteen hours.

Then we came to a place in Northern Illinois, where our guardian angels, and probably a few others, came to our rescue as a result of Mr. Olson's prayers. Bill and I arrived at the top of a long hill, which had a fairly sharp curve to the left at the bottom that led to a bridge over a small stream. The sides of the bridge were cement about three feet high and at least a foot thick. As we went down that hill gaining speed, we had no idea what lay ahead. All of a sudden, we were at the bottom of the hill and into the curve. The centrifugal force of our speed, combined with our body weight of about 340 pounds, plus our luggage, was more than Bill could handle. He tried to keep the cycle in the center of our lane. Although we leaned to the left, the bike went off the right edge of the road heading straight for the side of the bridge. Somehow we went by that bridge without touching it. In my mind, I pictured how the crash bar on the motorcycle had passed by the side of the bridge with only two or three inches to spare, probably only the thickness of our guardian angel's hand. We kept going, although slower, realizing that if we'd hit that bridge we'd now be in eternity.

I recently asked Bill how fast he thought we were going. He said, "I glanced at the speedometer after we passed the bridge, and it was close to ninety miles per hour."

The rest of our trip was essentially uneventful, although we were quite cautious about going down long hills. I remember that because we were driving in the evening hours, there were a lot of bugs hitting us and the windshield, feeling like small pellets. As we drove across southern Minnesota, we grew quite tired and, finally, at 12:30 a.m., stopped at a motel.

The next day was another beautiful day and we arrived safely home by noon. Our parents had been wondering how we were getting home as they didn't have a clue about our plans. Dad recorded in his diary on June 11, 1954, *"Bill and Dave home on a motorcycle at 12:35 p.m.!"* What he didn't record was his and Mom's emotional reaction to seeing us on that bike. As we pulled into the driveway, Bill revved up the motor and beeped the horn, announcing our arrival. Dad and Mom came running out of the house with an incredible look of shock and surprise on their faces.

Mom broke into tears. Dad, with a disgusted and angry look, said something I'll never forget: "The Lord watches over fools and drunkards!"

However, later that day, after we unwound, Bill showed Dad his proud possession, and Dad took it for a spin.

That summer Bill thoroughly enjoyed driving his motorcycle. I rode it a few times but Dad was on it every chance he could get, even making several pastoral calls on church members while on that Harley 74.

In spite of our narrow escape from an untimely death on the way home, Bill was still a bit risky with his bike at times. He told me of the time when he gave his girlfriend, Shirley, a ride to town on a two-lane highway. The traffic was moving very slowly so he started to pass cars on the right. All of a sudden, the car just in front of him pulled over to the curb and parked. To avoid hitting the car, Bill took to the sidewalk, flying through a flower garden that had a two-foot picket fence around it, causing flowers and fence to fly everywhere. Shirley was hanging on for dear life. I don't think he stopped to repair the garden or apologize to the homeowner.

On Friday, September 3, Dad recorded in his diary, "*Help Bill pack cycle. Pray with him.*" The next day he recorded, "*Bill leaves at 6 a.m.! How we missed him.*"

Bill had an uneventful return trip to Wheaton, arriving the next day at 10 a.m. to start football. A friend drove me back to college in his car.

The saga of the motorcycle maniacs continued through the next year. Bill and I continued to room together our sophomore year, although we'd moved out of the dorm and into a private home. Bill had permission to keep his bike in a corner of their garage.

In the middle of October, Bill sustained a concussion playing football that left him with severe headaches and he had to drop out of school. He got a ride home by car and the cycle stayed in the garage over winter.

The next spring at the end of my school year, I decided to do Bill a favor and drive his cycle home. On a pleasant day near the end of May, I backed the Harley out of the garage, dusted it off, and tried to start it. I cranked it several times before finally getting it running. But I had forgotten what the dealer told Bill when he bought it, "This bike has a suicide clutch." Which meant that even if the engine was idling in neutral it could suddenly shift into gear on its own and take off. He'd cautioned Bill, "Always turn the engine off instead of letting it idle." One time the previous summer, Bill forgot that advice and he almost pinned Shirley to a wall.

So, sure enough, as I was standing beside the bike, letting it warm up, it suddenly took off and ran into the front of the garage and tipped over on its side. I was panic-stricken thinking Bill would kill me if I damaged his bike. I managed to get the bike upright, but was unable to restart it.

I called home and told Bill what had happened. Needless to say, he was quite upset thinking I had destroyed his cycle. I talked to Dad and he agreed to come to Wheaton with a trailer to carry the bike home. I'm sure that was divine intervention for my own safety, because who knows what bridge, or something else, I might have hit had I started out on my own.

Bill enjoyed riding his motorcycle around that summer of 1955, and so did Dad. Bill never bought a license for the bike since that piece of cardboard stating "license applied for" worked just fine. By fall, Bill's desire for a car overcame his desire for a motorcycle, so he traded it in on a '51 Ford. (The dealer who made the trade sold the bike to a farmer, who three weeks later lost control of the bike on a gravel road, hit a tree, destroyed the cycle, and was killed.)

The Dream of my Life

I had gone through a couple of "heartthrobs" in my last year of high school, but they'd been back in Minnesota, and gradually faded from my thoughts. In my first two years of college I did some dating but studies and work limited my social life.

One day near the end of my junior year, as I was going through the lunch line, I noticed a very attractive, Italian chick standing behind the service line passing out salads. She gave me a very nice smile, which I returned, and I thought, "Who is that gal? I'd like to meet her."

A few days later, while going through the lunch line again, I saw the young woman having lunch with a good friend and class-mate, Gordon Anderson. I nonchalantly took my tray over to their table and asked if I could join them. Gordon said, "Of course," and introduced me to his friend, Anna Toleno. I enjoyed our conversation, not realizing until many months later that Anna hadn't wanted me to join them. She was interested in Gordon, not me. When summer came we went our separate ways.

Our first date

That fall I tried to get a date with Anna. She seemed interested but was always working. She'd even given me her work schedule, but this absent-minded senior kept forgetting to look at it.

I finally learned Anna's work schedule and we had our first date, recorded in my diary as October 27, 1956. I took Anna to an artist series on campus that had a four-piano quartet. We had a wonderful time together and enjoyed more and more fun dates as the year rolled into 1957.

Romantic literature class

The first semester came to an end and we registered for the next one. I had to take a class in romantic literature to meet the requirements for graduation in May. Seniors always registered first, followed by the juniors, so I was fortunate to get into this class taught by an excellent professor, Dr. Kilby, because his classes filled fast.

When Anna learned that I was in Dr. Clyde Kilby's class she made a beeline to register for the same one. To her dismay, Dr. Kilby told her the class was already full. Anna pleaded with him to make an exception as she really needed to be in his class. To her joy, he relented and registered her, and we were delighted to be able to sit next to each other. We often wondered if Dr. Kilby saw the real reason why Anna "needed" to be in that class.

Exchanging rings

Our dating picked up in February, wanting to be together whenever possible. On February 15 I recorded in my diary, *"Picked Anna up after work (used my roommates car)—had long talk – committed it all to the Lord and He gave real peace—prayer together—decided not to see each other until Thursday."*

However, the very next day I recorded, *"I saw Anna tonight (couldn't wait until Thursday)—a real time of fellowship in Him—we exchanged rings and pictures—Psalm 34:1-5—started going steady with Anna Toleno."*

Washington Banquet

The highlight date for us, and most students and faculty, was the annual Washington Banquet near the end of February, held in the Conrad Hilton Banquet Room of the Sheraton Hotel in downtown Chicago. The theme of that year's banquet was "Author of Liberty." A faculty member and spouse were chosen to dress up as George and Martha Washington. The guest speaker was Mark Hatfield from Oregon, a remarkably young speaker of the state, who spoke on "Paths of Peace."

We triple dated with good friends and everyone came dressed to the hilt in tuxes, beautiful gowns, and wearing appropriate flowers with their attire. My closing diary remark was, *"Anna was beautiful!!!"*

Anna "The Poet"

One night in the spring I was working in the railroad tower in Wheaton. Anna and I both had a big romantic literature test the next day. Fortunately, I was able to study between trains passing. But that night Anna had given me an envelope with instructions to open it at 2 a.m. When I opened it I found this poem. The title, To My Sleepy Eyes, by Anna Toleno.

Dear Sleepy Eyes:
(The one I prize)
How do you feel, my sweet?

Are you awake
This book to take,
And ere the test complete?

For with the dawn
The time is gone
For you to get it beat.

So study hard
About the bard,
Whose name I shain't repeat.

These poets are the luckiest,
For they have you, I only rest.
And with these lines I'd best retreat.

A lady should be somewhat shy,
In what she writes down to her guy,
So, I'll just say "good-night"—my sweet!

P.S. Beloved, I forgot to say—
I love you on this new-born day,
With love that's grown a great deal more,
Than it was on the day before.

In mid-May we had Senior Sneak, where the seniors who wished were allowed to slip away from campus and take the bus to the Jack and Jill Ranch in Wisconsin.

I decided to fake my sweetheart out. I asked for a date to a movie Thursday night, but told her I needed a nap in the afternoon, which allowed me to sneak away. I wrote her a note telling her I was gone for the weekend and my roommate delivered it to her after I left. I had a lot of fun with our classmates over the weekend as we anticipated graduation and moving on in life.

I had this poem waiting for me when I returned.

"To the Man Who Ran"
By I. B. Mad
You snuck away behind my back,
By taking off for the railroad track.
I hope you rode the CAE,
But if you didn't, it's alright with me!

Now the weekend's past.
You've returned at last!
Too bad it was so brief—
The absence was a relief!

I must confess
I enjoyed the rest.
No slaps on my cheek,
Nor stomps on my feet.

But now that you're here,
I must say, my dear,
Before I will speak
Back to me you must sneak!

Later at the end of June after my graduation, I received another very touching poem from Anna.

"Just Dave"
There is a man that I love dear,
No matter if he's far or near.
Around my neck I wear his ring,
From the giant finger of my little king.

Though he may not sit on a throne of gold—
To me he's a knight both brave and bold.
He stands above the rest of the crowd,
Has a quiet voice—though it's loud.

His shoulders are broad and his chest is firm,
One look at him and a Tarzan would squirm.
His hair is dark and his eyes the same,
He's sometimes rough, but most time tame.

When he smiles at me I melt like butter,
I really can't help it—by heart's a-flutter.
He's handsome and strong, and I love this man,
I love him as much as I feel I can—

Yet moment by moment my love grows stronger,
'Til sometimes I feel I can bear it no longer.
There are many reasons I love him so—
The way he walks—his radiant glow.

But the most important thing I can say,
Is he walks with God in a wondrous way.
My Master and his are one and the same,
And to serve Him on earth is our common aim.

That's the reason the love, which we share, is so sweet,
For it came from much prayer at the Master's feet.
Now you know why this one man I adore,
The Lord gave me him—could I ask for much more?

—The one who loves Him and him,
Anna

Farewell for the summer

My graduation was in the first part of June and it was a great time for Anna to meet my family. My dad and mom, sister, brother and his wife, and my aunt and uncle were all with us. Anna was a big hit!

I landed two good jobs in the Wheaton area for the summer, while Anna had an excellent waitress position near her hometown of Tenafly, New Jersey. It was hard to say goodbye so we kept the mailman busy. The end of August came quickly and I went into Chicago to a recommended jewelry store where I purchased a certain set of rings. I also bought a train ticket to Grand Central Station in Manhattan, ten miles from Anna's home.

It was my turn to meet her family and friends. I felt warmly welcomed by everyone. We visited Lake Sebago, a beautiful place in New York, and enjoyed the beach and walking trails.

The week went by too fast. Soon it was time to go back to Wheaton, pack up my worldly goods, including the special rings, and return to Minnesota, to start medical school at the University of Minnesota.

Medical School

In early August, I received a nice letter from my Aunt Eleanor. She and her husband, Len, lived in South Minneapolis and invited me to live with them while I was in medical school. They had a nicely furnished basement with a bed, table, and other furniture. Knowing it would be a great place to live and study, I gratefully said, "Yes."

Year one

Medical school started Monday, the last day of September, with a three-hour convocation in the morning. In the afternoon I had an a one-hour anatomy lecture, followed by three hours of anatomy lab where two classmates and I received a cadaver and began to, as my diary says, *"Dissect skin from the thigh. Ugh!"*

On my second day of classes, I entered the following in my diary, *"Studied. All of a sudden I realize how much I have to study—WOW!—Took home bones to study."*

Three days later I had another diary entry, *"Devotions—classes all day—boy, this is really rugged—seems like I won't make it—but with the Lord's strength I will."*

Soon I was blessed by meeting a Christian physician, Dr. Sponsal, at Lake Harriet Baptist Church, where I attended. He took a real interest in me, even inviting me to follow him around his office and observe while he saw patients. That proved to be a great experience.

I became active in the Christian Medical Society present on campus where I met other believers a year or two ahead of me. That gave everyone a sense of community and encouragement.

School went smoothly after the initial shock. Devotions in the morning, classes, labs, and study, study, study. I found I was really enjoying what I was doing. However, the biggest highlight for me was getting letters from Anna, to which I quickly wrote back, and the occasional phone calls. I was really excited to learn that she was going to come up to Minneapolis for Thanksgiving. My Aunt Eleanor had invited all our family, and Anna, to be at her and Len's house for Thanksgiving. I couldn't wait!

Engagement, wedding, and honeymoon

The day before Thanksgiving, Anna rode home with a couple of other Wheatonites who lived in Minneapolis. Although they couldn't leave the school until late afternoon, I stayed up until she arrived at 3 a.m., Thursday morning. We talked a long time. I was originally going to ask for her hand in marriage during Christmas when she'd be at our home in Laverne. But I couldn't wait. I went to my special drawer, took out the diamond ring, walked back to her, knelt, and said, "Anna, would you please marry me?" In my diary I recorded, "*Totally surprised her. Oh for a camera and tape recorder!*"

Later in the day after everyone had gathered at Len and Eleanor's home, Anna put on her black cashmere coat and walked around with her left hand on her right shoulder, with the diamond sparkling against the black background. Finally, Shirley, my brother Bill's wife, saw it and shouted, "Anna, what's that thing on your finger?" All eyes immediately focused on her hand. There were expressions of excitement and joy over the wonderful surprise.

That weekend went by very fast and we began planning our wedding with great joy and anticipation. Once Anna left, I looked at my medical school calendar and realized that my first year didn't end until my final exam, Friday morning, July 18, 1958. The wedding was to be in Grace Chapel in Tenafly, New Jersey. This meant that the earliest we could get married was Monday, July 21. So that became our special day.

I had a week off from medical school the end of March, so I hitchhiked to Wheaton—took me ten hours—for a very special celebration.

On Saturday evening, several friends were thrilled to be allowed to ring the Wheaton College tower bell, while Anna and I stood in the tower next to the bell. (I think that's why later in life I've lost some of my hearing.) Then we had a wonderful party at Dr. Gordon and Dorothea Jaeck's home with our friends.

Another important event occurred mid-May when I purchased a 1952 Pontiac, my first car. I knew that having my own transportation would be essential in the next couple of months.

During the first week of June, between Anna's last final exam at Wheaton and her graduation, she took the train to Minneapolis. We met and went apartment hunting, finding what we needed on Como Avenue, close to the University of Minnesota campus. Anna also had several job interviews.

Anna's major was sociology so she was looking for a job in that field. She had a wonderful resource in one of her professors, Dr. Gordon Jaeck, who had been chairman of the Minnesota State Parole Board before taking a teaching position at Wheaton College. While Anna drove the Pontiac around to the various interviews, I studied.

Finally in mid-June, Anna learned she had gotten a job as a probation officer with Ramsey County, starting September 1, 1958. We both were excited and grateful.

We returned to Wheaton for Anna's graduation. Her parents drove in from New Jersey, arriving Saturday afternoon. Anna was thrilled that they were able to make the drive. Because it was a rainy weekend, commencement was indoors. The next day we went our separate ways, with Anna returning with her parents to New Jersey to get things ready for our wedding. I returned to Minneapolis with most of Anna's things in the Pontiac.

After my final exam on Friday morning, July 18, I hopped in the Pontiac and drove 1,300 miles straight through to Anna's home in New Jersey, arriving about 8:30 a.m., Saturday morning. My dad and mom, and sister, Jeannie, had already arrived. Bill, my best man, and Shirley, flew in later that day. My Uncle Len and Aunt Eleanor came on Sunday.

Grace Chapel graciously allowed Dad to perform our ceremony. My groomsmen were two of Anna's brothers, Bill and Larry Toleno. Her bridesmaids were a good friend, Rita Smevberg, and my sister, Jeannie. The service was simply beautiful. We stayed calm and thoroughly enjoyed everything. Anna's relatives were very impressed.

Anna had planned our honeymoon, taking us into Upstate New York to various beautiful spots. Then we were to spend two days on Monhegan Island, Maine, a small, rocky island, ten miles from the nearest mainland, and scarcely a square mile in area, accessible only by boat.

Unfortunately, we were a little late arriving for our scheduled ride out to the island, so we had to hire a fisherman with a small boat to take us. He carried a barrel of rotten redfish that he used for lobster bait and, boy, did it stink! But it was an unexpected experience that brought laughter and fond memories.

We enjoyed two days of hiking in the various trails and observing the various artists who were painting the beauty of the wilderness areas.

Next we went into New Brunswick, Canada, Quebec, and

Ontario, stopping at various interesting places. We came back into the US at Niagara Falls, thoroughly enjoying the spectacular views.

Finally, except for a couple of flat tires, we leisurely made our way back to Minneapolis, and to our first home at 1919 Como Avenue Southeast.

Three more years

The last three years of medical school were much different from my first year, primarily because I was married. Anna thoroughly enjoyed being a probation officer and often shared with me interesting stories from her job. We both were grateful that her income put me through med school.

Anna and I became active in Hope Baptist Church in South Minneapolis. We helped out with the youth group, led by Doug and Norma Madison, good friends of ours from Wheaton College days.

As I advanced in medical knowledge and skill I was able to get part-time jobs at various hospitals. My first job at North Memorial Hospital was doing history and physicals on patients admitted from the emergency room. I also worked in the ER under the supervision of one of the residents, which further advanced my skill and knowledge.

In my senior year, I began thinking about where I would like to take an internship. I was sure that I wanted to be a family physician, but at that time a resident program had not yet been established for that. I only needed a one-year internship before I could go into a practice. I knew I wanted an internship that would give me as much hands-on experience as possible, so I and several classmates applied to Anchor Hospital in St. Paul. I was pleased to be accepted with a starting time of July 1, 1961.

Besides being accepted for internship, another very important event happened in our lives during my senior year. Seven and a half months before my graduation on June 10, Anna announced that she was pregnant with our first child. That was very exciting and thrilling for both of us. She was able to work almost up to the time she delivered, which was on July 27, 1961. Our firstborn son, Dan, entered the world at St. Joseph's Hospital and the delivering doctor used a "brain altering" gas to help with her labor pains. Her first comment after Dan was born was, "What did I have, a loaf of bread?"

My Internship

My rotating internship was a great training experience for me as it took me through surgery, OB-GYN, internal medicine, orthopedics, and many other significant specialties. I spent a large amount of time working in the emergency room improving my skills in dealing with all kinds of trauma and medical emergencies. I also worked extra time in surgery, preparing for a small-town practice in family medicine, which was my desire. At the end of the year I felt my internship had been very educational and stimulating, even though exhausting (twenty-four hours straight at a time). I felt well-prepared for my first medical practice.

After the one year of internship, I originally planned to apply for a US Public Health Service position, probably in North Dakota, where I would work in an Indian hospital, satisfying my two-year military obligation. I had already applied for this when I got a phone call from a good friend of mine, Dr. Dick Rowe, in January 1962.

Dick was a year ahead of me in medical school. He and his wife, I'Anne, were good Christian friends. We'd both been active in the student chapter of the Christian Medical Society on the University of Minnesota Medical School campus. Dick called to invite us for a weekend visit to Littlefork, a small town in Northern Minnesota, located just south of International Falls, Minnesota, three hundred miles from the Twin Cities. Following his year of internship the previous July, Dick had joined a medical practice in Littlefork with Dr. Roger MacDonald.

With the Rowes being close friends, we thought a weekend away from the rigors of internship would be a good break. So we packed up our first child, six-month-old Daniel, plus all the items we needed, into our Volkswagen on a cold Friday morning in February and headed north. Six hours later we arrived tired, but happy to see our friends.

What Dick neglected to tell me in his phone call, was that there was a reception for us in the local hospital on Saturday evening.

When we arrived at the meeting place, we were shocked to see, waiting to greet us, every "significant" person in this town of 960. We quickly learned that there was a lot more to this weekend visit than just spending time with our good friends. Dr. MacDonald was leaving Littlefork for another practice north of Duluth, Minnesota, and my friend, Dick, along with the town people, were anxiously looking for a replacement. To say the least, we were quite taken back, but we assured Dick and I'Anne, we would pray about it.

Anna and I returned to the cities, perplexed and wondering. However, as we sought divine direction for our lives, we sensed that God wanted us in Littlefork for the next step in our journey. I withdrew my application to the US Public Health Service and said yes to Dick and the town of Littlefork.

4

Enjoying Life
as a Country Doc

It was exciting and challenging to join a partnership practice in a small, Northern Minnesota town. Because there was a hospital there, my partner and I were able to practice the full level of family medicine as we had been trained.

On July 3, Dick Stapleton arrived from Littlefork with a truck and trailer to help us move our small amount of earthly possessions to this small, but beautiful town. This started another wonderful episode in our lives together, and we were thrilled as we pulled into Littlefork to join Dr. Dick Rowe in the practice of medicine.

We rented a two-bedroom, one-bathroom home. There was a small but nice clinic building adequate for two doctors. Since there was no pharmacy in town, the closest one being in International Falls twenty miles away, we ended up with our own pharmacy in the clinic to fill our prescriptions. The clinic building was owned by the hospital that also employed us.

The hospital was rather tiny, but had an operating room, delivery room, and six to eight beds. Although a couple of years later, with the help of federal dollars through the Hill Burton Act, a new twenty-bed modern hospital was built.

The Start of Life in Littlefork

As we settled in, I reflected over the medical path I'd taken over the past ten years. I'd frequently dreamed of practicing medicine in a little town, in part, because I grew up in the country and small towns. And Littlefork fit me to a "T."

The shock of grocery shopping

After getting partially settled in Otto Imhoff's rental home, Anna, Dan, and I went to get groceries for our bare cupboards. Anna had only shopped in cities, so when we entered Wayne and Ralph Morris's Grocery Store she was totally taken aback, never having seen such a small store. Her first thought was, "How can I find anything here?" She looked at me as if to say, "Why did you bring me to such a small town?"

As she stood, stunned, I started putting things in our cart, saying, "We've got to buy something to eat." Gradually she joined me and we finished our first shopping experience in Littlefork. Actually, there was a good supply of everything needed, and in time, she adjusted to the smallness of our new location.

My salary

When we had visited Littlefork and received the surprise invitation to join Dick Rowe nothing was said about salary. Even when I said, "Yes," I had no idea of the level of my income. During my internship, I had received a hundred dollars a month, but I was sure it would exceed that. When I sat down with the hospital board to sign the contract with them I was told I would be paid a thousand dollars per month.

I was shocked. I couldn't believe my salary would be that much!

Deer hunting

Dick Stapleton and a couple of other men from the church we attended, usually hunted together. Since all I had hunted while growing up was rabbits or squirrels, I was excited to be invited to go deer hunting with them that first fall. One of them loaned me a gun and I did some target practice in preparation.

On the opening day, Anna was somewhat anxious to see me leave the house dressed in my hunting attire, carrying a gun. I assured her I would be okay and gave her a kiss as I left.

We drove to the hunting site in the early morning while still dark. The guys placed me on a deer stand, saying, "Make sure you don't fire the gun until a half hour after sunrise." They went on to a distant place in the woods, planning to walk slowly toward me, hoping to drive a deer into an open area near my location.

As I sat on my stand, I was amazed and a bit concerned at the number of times I heard gunshots off in the distance, well before sunrise. However, an hour or so after sunrise, a deer came into the open spot by my stand. My shot was accurate and I had my first deer. The other men soon arrived and were happy to see my success. We hunted through the day, unaware of a tragedy in another area away from town.

A good friend, Ray Gilmore, had invited two of his wife, Elsie's, brothers, to their deer hunting place. Ray directed them to two stands, well away from each other, planning to drive over after the legal opening for hunting deer. He gave them strict instructions, "Sit still and don't shoot when you hear a thing unless you have a clear line of sight."

Sadly, while it was still dark, one of the brothers got out of his stand and started walking around. The other brother, hearing the sound, shot in that direction, fatally hitting his brother in the chest.

The news of what happened was all over town by 10 a.m., and when Anna heard the news she was beside herself, fearing for my safety. She was greatly relieved when I walked in the door much later in the day.

Some Experiences in my Medical Practice

Three-year-old with a problem

One humorous visit occurred shortly after starting my practice. A lady brought her son to the clinic from the neighboring town of Bigfork. He had pushed a pea up his nose, and in a state of panic, she rushed him into the office. As I recall, the pea was in the left nostril, rather far up where I couldn't reach it with a forceps. So I applied pressure over the right nostril and told the child to blow hard. With one blow, out popped the pea into my hand.

The mom was surprised and exclaimed, "I could have done that myself! Are you going to charge me?"

I smiled, thinking, "Knowing what to do has value." But I responded, "No, this is a freebie."

Most common injury

Logging was the main industry in that area, due to the paper mill at International Falls. The loggers used sharp chainsaws to cut the trees down, trim off the branches, and cut them into appropriate lengths. They handled them with care and respect. Still, chainsaw cuts were quite common, especially on the leg. It wasn't unusual for a logger to come in with two or three fresh cuts. The saw would hit a knot or something else on the tree, jump to his leg, and literally start marching upwards, leaving two or three significant lacerations, all happening quickly.

My job was to thoroughly clean and close the wound. I became pretty good at taking care of the lacerations and preventing follow-up infections.

Busy day in the delivery room

Obstetrics was not a big part of our practice, but it was one I always enjoyed, regardless of the time, day or night. And in May

1963, we were anticipating a special day with the birth of our second child.

My partner, Dick Rowe, was Anna's doctor. He owned a small plane that he flew into Canada to do medical mission work among an Indian tribe at Lac la Croix, usually going for a day or two every other week.

Anna went into labor during the very early hours of May 14. As the day passed we realized she was in true labor. We knew Dick was planning on making one of his trips in the morning of the same day. I quickly called him before he left his home and told him he would need to postpone leaving for a few hours.

He gladly agreed and delivered our Deborah at 11:58 a.m.

Later that afternoon, I had the privilege of delivering twin boys, Glen and Gordon Dobbs. I was sure glad they both came out head first.

But that wasn't the end. That evening I had a third delivery, another boy. This was quite an unusual experience to have four new babies in the Littlefork Hospital nursery.

Solo practice for eight months

In the third year of our partnership, which had been going very well, Dick gave me some unwelcome news. He felt led to relocate to another practice in Silver Bay, Minnesota, north of Duluth. That was a shock to both of us, but our only recourse was to pray and begin looking for another partner.

I knew of a Christian friend, Joel Brende, who'd been a couple of years behind me in medical school. I asked him and his wife, Marilyn, to consider joining us. They checked out the practice and agreed to come. That was a big answer to prayer!

However, there was an eight-month period where I was in solo practice. It wasn't that I was busy twenty-four-seven, but the fact that I had to be available all the time was an undesirable responsibility. I continued to take a half-day off weekly, but usually didn't get home until 2 p.m., or later, on those days.

Sometimes our family would go to International Falls for various reasons. I had a two-way radio to communicate with the hospital, the only problem being no reception when I was in town. So I had to keep going to the southern edge of town in order to check in and see if all was quiet.

One sunny Saturday afternoon, we were with friends picnicking and swimming on Lake Kapetogama, about twenty miles to the east, when my radio went off. The nurse reported that a sick child needed to be seen ASAP. I hopped into our VW, knowing Anna and the kids would ride home with friends. It was dusk and the road had two lanes, trees lining both sides of the road, twenty feet away. I was probably driving a bit faster than I should when "Bang!" something hit the passenger side of the VW. I looked to my left and saw a deer staggering into the trees. I stopped and could hear thrashing noise in the woods. But at that point there was nothing I could do, so I continued a bit slower to the hospital, where I reported this incident to the DNR (Department of National Resources).

"Anesthesiologist" for Littlefork and International Falls Hospitals

During my internship, after deciding to go to Littlefork, I had spent extra time with anesthesiologists hoping to improve my knowledge and skill in that area of medicine.

At Littlefork Hospital, I began giving anesthesia, especially after the new hospital was built in 1964. My new partner, Dr. Brende, was equally skilled. When the International Falls doctors learned of what we were doing at Littlefork they asked us to do the same for them, to which we gladly complied.

Serving in the First Baptist Church

We were blessed to have a pastor and his wife, John and Nancy Redmond, whom we enjoyed and respected. They were with us in the church most of the time that we were in Littlefork, and became lifelong friends.

We loved being involved in our church in a variety of ways, including teaching classes and serving on various church boards. Anna also led the Vacation Bible School every summer. But what we enjoyed most was serving as youth sponsors for the ninth through twelfth grades. We led their group in regular Bible studies, had various camping experiences, along with just hanging out with them whenever possible.

On three different occasions we took four or five juniors on a trip to Trinity College, Moody Bible Institute, and Wheaton College, wanting to expose them to some good Christian schools. We were thrilled when two from the Stapleton family, Russ and Mary, ended up going to Wheaton College.

The Growth of our Family

Following the birth of Dan and Deb, we were blessed to have three more children. Becky had the dubious honor of being the first New Year's baby at Littlefork Hospital. She was born February 23, 1965, and was given three beautiful roses in token of her birth on that day.

Anna's next pregnancy only lasted five months when the fetus died in utero. Why? Only God knows. We grieved the loss of Timothy William, but knew we'll meet him in heaven.

Melanie was born May 3, 1968, covered with black hair. She had more Italian blood in her from her mother than the other kids. And oh, how she loved to play in mud puddles.

Our last, but not least, child came seven years later after we relocated to Golden Valley, Minnesota. Matthew William was born March 6, 1975. What a joy to have another son.

We enjoyed our busy life in Littlefork, becoming involved in community life in various ways. I was elected to the school board for a three-year term, which was interesting, challenging, and very worthwhile. I also played basketball with a group of men who enjoyed shooting hoops.

Though we were pleased with life where we were, I had three periods of time during our seven years there, when I prayerfully wondered, "Is this to be a long-term location for us as a family or does God have something else for us?" Following the first two periods of wondering and praying about it, we felt peace that we should stay put. However, the third time was different.

My mom was a real intercessor in prayer for her family, friends, missionaries, et cetera. At that time, she and Dad lived in Parkers Prairie, Minnesota, where dad pastored the First Baptist Church. Mom sensed that God had something else for us, so she began to pray that "God would stir up the nest," which is exactly what He did.

5

The Call to
a Third World Country

I had a growing desire to spend a year or more practicing medicine in a third world country. I felt that would help clarify for us whether we should pursue full-time service abroad or stay in a small-town practice in Minnesota, and my wife was in agreement. It was exciting to see how God orchestrated the entire process that brought us to a mission hospital in Africa.

I n the fall of 1967, Anna and I again began to feel a little unsettled. We couldn't figure out why, but we sensed God was up to something. We began questioning whether Littlefork was the long term place for us and prayed for discernment and clarity. We'd been thinking about building our own home, but with the uncertainty we were feeling, we put those thoughts on hold.

In February 1968, we started to probe a little by visiting a Christian doctor friend of mine, Dr. Ernie Lorentzen, and his practice in Detroit Lakes, Minnesota, who was looking for a partner. We had a delightful visit with Dr. Lorentzen and his wife and were impressed with the clinic and the town. But we returned to Littlefork with a clear sense that that was not the place for us. So our wondering and prayer for discernment continued.

Some Interesting Happenings

A visit

An unusual thing happened in early March 1968. A dear friend, Andy Anderson, a pharmacist in International Falls, knowing of our interest in the mission field called us, wondering if we would like to meet a missionary speaker, Irving Philgreen, the assistant director of Short Terms Abroad, who was speaking in his church. STA was an organization designed to arrange for interested people to go to the mission field for a short time. They had a new concept available to those who were unsure about long-term mission work but were willing to try a year or two.

Mr. Philgreen came to our home that same afternoon. We found it very encouraging to hear about the medical opportunities abroad for only one year. Right in the middle of our conversation, the telephone rang.

A timely phone call

On the other end of the phone was Dr. Bob Cullen, a family physician from Elmore, Minnesota. He had heard through the grapevine of drug representatives, who call on physicians, that I might be looking for another practice. I assured him that I wasn't interested in leaving Littlefork unless it was to go abroad in a medical missionary capacity. Since he was the medical director of the Conservative Baptist Foreign Missionary Society he urged me to consider the Missionary Assistance Corps program, sponsored by CBFMS. The amazing aspect of this phone call was that Dr. Cullen said he'd had my name on his desk for a lengthy period of time, but hadn't felt led to call me until that very afternoon.

Anna and I felt this was no coincidence since we were visiting with Mr. Philgreen about short-term medical work.

An interesting newsletter

In July 1968, my folks mailed me a CBFMS paper describing Dr. Cullen and his wife, Jean's, decision to go to Ruanguba Hospital in Eastern Congo. We did a double-take, wondering if his phone call in March was not so much an invitation to join him in Elmore but, rather, at Ruanguba Hospital in Congo. We knew God was clearly working in our lives and we would ultimately know His will.

Other opportunities for service abroad, especially with Dr. Wendell and Margie Geary in Borneo, turned out to be closed doors.

However, one other incredible experience played a role in our decision.

Divine Intervention on Trip to Wheaton, Illinois

The Christian Medical and Dental Society was holding a three-day medical missionary conference at Wheaton College the following Christmas in 1968. Anna and I thought this would be a good opportunity to receive clarity about our possible service abroad. We were able to leave our four children with capable, good friends in Littlefork and fly to Chicago.

Our flight was grounded in Green Bay due to bad weather over Chicago. We tried to get on the next flight coming from Minneapolis to Green Bay and then on to Chicago. Although several people on our plane were able to secure a seat, four people in front of us they stopped taking further passengers. The plane was North Central Airlines, flight 458. Rather than stay overnight in Green Bay, we rented a car and invited four college students, who were on the original flight from International Falls, to ride with us and share expenses.

We were halfway to Chicago when a sudden news report came on the radio, stating that flight 458 had crashed trying to land at Midway Airport in Chicago. There were forty-one passengers and a crew of four. Thirty-one passengers were killed. We knew that

God's guardian angels had protected us, and we were incredibly grateful.

We also realized that God had more "good works" for us to do, not the least of which was to parent our four children. Ephesians 2:10 (NASB) came to mind, "*For we are His workmanship created in Christ Jesus for good works, which God prepared beforehand so that we would walk in them.*"

Decision Made

As other doors closed, the door to Ruanguba, Congo, remained open. Communications with Dr. Cullen confirmed that, indeed, his phone call to me the previous March was, in fact, an invitation to join him at Ruanguba. We felt great peace that this was the direction God had for us.

Then the incredible task started of preparing ourselves and our four children, ages eight, six, four, and six months for the experience of a lifetime.

Preparations to Leave for Africa

Telling my partner

I had said nothing to my partner, Dr. Brende, about our possibly leaving. And he had said nothing to me of his thoughts of leaving our family practice and taking up a residency program in psychiatry. So when Anna and I made our decision, he was the first one I told. Then he told me what he'd been thinking.

As it turned out, Dr. Brende was able to enroll in a residency program in June of 1969. So he left Littlefork before we did.

Notifying the hospital board

My next step was to notify the hospital board at Littlefork that we would be leaving on or around August 1, 1969. That came as a big shock since my partner had already notified them of his plans to leave. This was especially hard for the board, as well as the town, to lose both of their doctors,which meant the hospital had to close until they could find another physician.

Clothing for the kids and Italian spaghetti

Anna and I began making lists of various items, especially clothing that we would need. We corresponded with different missionaries at Ruanguba, and received good suggestions from them. Since we packed with the possibility of staying two years, we had to guess at how much the kids would grow in order to bring the appropriate clothing and shoes. We packed a total of nine barrels and two crates. Of course, one of the barrels was filled with Italian spaghetti and all its ingredients as Anna wanted some good "home cooking" on occasion. One crate held a refrigerator and the other, a freezer. A third crate carrying an old-fashioned ringer washing machine would be sent from where we'd ordered it in Chicago.

One thing we didn't realize at the time, however, was the barrels and crates wouldn't show up at our Congo home until three months after we had arrived. We were "dying" for some Italian spaghetti by then.

Immunizations

One of the unpleasant aspects of this preparation was all the immunizations we needed for our own protection. The kids were excited about our trip but didn't like seeing me come home in the evening with a handful of syringes. Becky was the most frightened one—if I came in the front door, she would run out the back. If I tried to sneak in the back door, she'd hear me and out the front she'd go. But eventually all the shots were given.

Storage and other things

Because this was a relatively short-term mission trip we had to store all of our furniture and other belongings with friends, since we would need them when we returned from the mission field. We were able, however, to sell our boat and station wagon. Our new pastor, Wes Thompson, was kind enough to agree to rent out our house and look after any problems that might arise while we were gone.

After five months of preparation, we were finally ready to embark on this new adventure. Now it was time to say goodbye.

Bon Voyage

Farewell to Littlefork

August 3 was a Sunday and a very big day for us. My dad and mom, along with my sister, Jeannie, her husband, Vern, and their two children, Pam and Tim, were able to take part in some of the morning and evening services at First Baptist Church in which we'd been in charge.

The community farewell service was held in the high school in the afternoon. There were a large number of people from the town and surrounding areas in attendance. It was heartwarming, yet sad, to say goodbye to so many friends and coworkers from the church and the hospital. A basket of cards was presented to us that contained many fond expressions, as well as monetary gifts.

Time with Anna's family

The next morning we boarded a plane to Newark, New Jersey, where we spent a week with Anna's family. We were glad for the time we had with them, although they didn't approve of us going so far away.

On August 11, Anna's parents, along with three of her siblings, Tom, Gary, and Susan, took us to JFK Airport for our departure.

We flew out in the evening for London, arriving there the next morning. We slept a few hours in a motel, then had a quick taxi tour of London. Next we flew to Frankfurt, Germany, for a short layover. Finally, we flew into Entebbe, Uganda, arriving August 13 at 7:45 a.m. That was quite the experience as our plane came in for a landing. All we could see out our windows was dense forest or jungle. We said to each other, "Hope there's a runway out here somewhere." Then all of a sudden, there was a break in the trees and we landed safely.

Dr. Bob Cullen met us at the airport with his son, John. We drove to Kampala, Uganda. We spent August 13 and 14 getting supplies, including bikes and trikes for the kids. We left Kampala early in the morning of August 15, driving over horrible roads. We arrived at the mission station around 7 p.m., after being on the road for thirteen hours, completely exhausted. Across the road leading to the hospital was a big welcome sign that said, "Karibu, Dr. and Mrs. McQuoid." (*Karibu* is Swahili for welcome.) Thus began a wonderful year of many different experiences that we wouldn't change for anything.

6

The Challenge and Joy of Practicing Medicine Abroad

Practicing medicine in a third world country was very challenging. I had an older, experienced partner who was a great help. Often I was called upon to do surgical procedures well beyond my training simply because there was no one else to do it. Frequent guidance by my partner or a good textbook gave an acceptable outcome in most situations. In addition, it was a great privilege to travel in Eastern Congo, Uganda, and Kenya visiting many mission hospitals as well as seeing several beautiful animal parks.

The Ruanguba Mission Station was located in the eastern part of Congo, close to the border of Uganda. The Lorimer Memorial Hospital, Hannah Hunter Cole Memorial School for Grades 2–8, dormitories for the children, and the African Bible School were all located on this station. In addition, there were several homes where the missionaries lived.

Our location was in a mountainous region about seventy-five kilometers north of Goma, Congo, with an elevation of 6,500 feet. As we looked south from our yard we saw several volcanic mountains ranging from 11,000 to 14,800 feet in height. The most noted one was an active volcano, Mount Nyriagongo, which we climbed more than once during our year in Africa. The view was beautiful.

A very nice, unoccupied, two-story missionary home was awaiting our arrival. The first floor contained a kitchen with storage, a dining and living room with a fireplace, and an office where Anna held school for Debbie and Becky. There also were two bedrooms and a bathroom, with a long stairway leading to the bedrooms. The house was furnished fairly well with furniture left by previous missionaries.

We were filled with joy and peace as we looked with anticipation toward what lay ahead for us, confident we were where God wanted us.

Adjusting to a New Way of Life

We experienced a significant culture shock as we entered life in this new place. With the lack of conveniences that we'd enjoyed just four days prior we felt we were stepping back in time.

In addition, we'd arrived at a very difficult time. The generator that supplied electricity to the mission compound was out and wouldn't be repaired for more than a month. It was hard doing surgery at night using flashlights. We'd come at the peak of an unusually dry season, so the cistern, which supplied water to the house we were living in, was dry. That meant our hired help had to carry large buckets of water from a nearby river and empty them into a barrel next to our kitchen door. However, when there was adequate rain, the cistern filled up and we would pump water from it into two barrels that were on a deck attached to the side of the house at the second-floor level. Pipes from the barrels were attached to the faucets and toilet in the bathroom as well as the kitchen, giving a gravity fed water system in our house. Of course, we had to boil any water needed for cooking or drinking.

A further problem was that tree roots had plugged up the pipe to our septic tank so we had no toilet facilities. However, this situation lasted only about four days until repairs could be made.

Other significant adjustments were learning where to find different types of food, how to keep and prepare them, and attempting to learn a little Swahili so we could communicate with our help. A further change was doing our laundry in the bathtub for three months until the washer, which we'd ordered while in the States, arrived. Our fifteen-month-old Melanie was still in diapers, which compounded the problem.

Mail service was more reliable coming through the country of Uganda than through Congo. It was approximately twenty miles from our mission station to the Congo-Uganda border. Just across the border was the small town of Kisoro where the mail arrived and was picked up by someone from the mission. There was a nice store in the town run by an East Asian Indian whose name was Mr. Alalji. He was very helpful and well-liked by the missionaries.

Early on we knew we would have to purchase a vehicle for travel. Fortunately, I was able to buy a small Toyota station wagon in Goma shortly after our arrival, which proved to be an excellent choice for us.

In spite of the all those struggles we were grateful to be there, enjoying a slower pace of living. Interestingly, both Anna and I felt a sense of lightheartedness with the simplicity of our lifestyle in Congo, free of the entanglements of a more complex society. We recalled, as we got rid of material possessions in preparation for this experience, "It was like weights falling off our shoulders."

Schooling for our Kids

Danny, as he was called then, age eight, attended third grade at the school on the station. He had an excellent teacher, JoAnn Kyle, and did very well. JoAnn taught second through fourth grade, while Elfie Pruitt, another very capable teacher, taught fifth through eighth grade.

Debbie, age six, was a first-grader, and since the policy of the mission was for moms to teach their first grade child at home Anna had the privilege of being her home-school mom. She used correspondence materials from Calvert Christian School, located in North Carolina.

Becky, age four, sat in the same classroom with Debbie and essentially did kindergarten work. Anna was surprised when she realized Becky was learning to read, although from her vantage point Becky was seeing the books upside down. This upset Anna because the educational philosophy of that day was not to teach pre-school children how to read. It turned out not to hurt Becky at all.

Melanie, age one year and three months, played with toys and took naps. Her favorite place to play was in the sandbox I'd made for her on the porch.

The two older girls had school before noon, while the afternoon was essentially play time. We got the children a puppy and named her Princess. She was a lot of fun for our family during our year there.

The Medical Work

An overview

The Lorimer Hospital at Ruanguba was built in the late 1940s by Dr. Charles Trout. Additions were added as monies became available. The staff consisted of Dr. Robert Cullen, RN Pat Person, and several African certified nurses, along with nurses aides. There was also a chaplain who ministered to the spiritual needs of each patient.

Certain days were designated for surgery, although many emergency surgeries were done anytime, day or night. An out-patient clinic was open five days a week, usually with a long line of patients to be seen.

In addition, there were thirteen clinics located one to four days away from the hospital that were part of the medical outreach. Each clinic was run by a certified African nurse. Patients that were too ill and requiring hospitalization were carried on boards, or whatever their family and friends could put together, to bring them to the hospital. The patient's relatives would bring food along to prepare at the hospital for themselves and the patient, and slept in the bed with the patient or on the cement floor near the bed.

I was challenged by the need to do so much surgery. But I was so grateful for Dr. Cullen, who as an older family physician had served as a missionary doctor in the past. He was quite adept at different types of surgery and graciously taught me procedures I never would do in the United States. I also had access to surgical textbooks that were very helpful when, for example, I was repairing a harelip on a child. I did a lot of hernia repairs, caesarean-sections, appendectomies, thyroid goiters, some bowel obstructions, and drained many, many abscesses.

My daily schedule, when not doing surgery, was to make rounds on hospital patients in the morning, followed by hours of seeing clinic patients. Frequently there were emergency interruptions.

Dr. Cullen and I took turns visiting one or more of the outlying thirteen clinics. The African nurse at each of the clinics would save up the more difficult patients for us to see when we were scheduled to visit that clinic.

My own surgery

I even got to experience my own surgery while in Congo. We had just arrived back from a three-week trip to Kenya, visiting some missionary friends. The day after I began working in the hospital, I developed right lower quadrant pain that went on to become an acute appendicitis. Dr. Cullen was preparing to visit some of the outlying clinics, but I called him on the mission station phone and told him that I needed to be checked by him first.

Dr. Cullen agreed with my diagnosis and I crawled onto the surgical table in the operating room, where he gave me a spinal anesthetic, which initially I thought was working. However, as he got through the outer layers of my abdomen I began to feel a great deal of pain. Anna said she could hear me groaning from the waiting room outside the OR where she and another missionary were praying.

I was very grateful that they had an ether gas machine that was easily operated by one of the nurses. So they switched me to ether and that's the last I remember until I woke up. Surgery was successful and I had a good recovery, except for two days with a spinal headache, which was totally unnecessary since the spinal didn't work. But such is life, especially in a third world country.

As we approached mid-December we became excited about a trip to Nairobi, Kenya, with no idea what lay before us. We were certainly glad that God knew and He had His guardian angels on the job.

Christmas with the Grovers

The start of our trip

We connected with good friends from Northern Minnesota, Dale and Vollie Grover, and their five children who were missionaries in Nairobi. They invited us to spend Christmas with them, which we were excited to do. Our plan was to leave December 16, spend the first night in Kampala, the capital of Uganda, and reach Nairobi the next day. However, I was concerned about one part of the trip, which was driving on the correct side of the road at all times. In Congo and Kenya, driving was on the right side, but in Uganda, it was on the left. As we started out, I asked Anna and the kids to keep reminding me to "think left" when driving in Uganda. The roads in Congo and most of Uganda were either gravel or mud. As we crossed over into Uganda I kept repeating to myself, "Think left."

Our mishap

We went through Kisoro and the road took us up a hill with a curve at the top, barely wide enough for two cars to pass each other. I was driving on the left-hand side and just as we arrived at the curved top a car came down the middle of the road. There was no time to think and I automatically reacted, moving to the right. The result was a head-on crash. Fortunately, neither of us were going very fast. Some of the kids in the backseat ended up in the front seat but we were grateful that no one was seriously hurt. Debbie ended up with a black and blue eye that lasted a few days.

The driver of the other car had a cut on his forehead that was bleeding briskly. A large number of local African people rapidly came out of the woodwork, shouting and looking very angrily at us. We'd been forewarned that if you're ever passing through a village and you hit a child as he runs in front of you, don't stop! Just keep on driving because the villagers will blame you and even kill you.

I wanted to get out and help the driver with the cut fore-head but was afraid to do so for fear of what the gathering, angry crowd might do to me. It was then that we experienced a "divine appearance."

Mr. Alalji, the owner of the store in Kisoro, just happened to be coming behind us. He immediately began talking to the gathering crowd in their language, quieting them down. He hooked up a rope from his car to ours and pulled us back to Kisoro. From there we were able to get a tow back to the mission station. With the help of fellow missionaries we soon got the radiator patched and a few other things fixed so we could resume our trip.

Uganda President shot

Two days later we were on the road again, driving ever so care-fully uphill and around curves. We safely drove to Masaka, Uganda, on the west side of Lake Victoria, where we stayed in a hotel. The next day we arrived at Kampala, Uganda.

As we settled into a missionary guesthouse and were getting ready for bed, sirens suddenly went off, with a lot of screaming and shouting going on outside. We didn't know what had happened until the next morning, but someone had attempted an assassination of President Obote of Uganda. He was struck by a bullet in the side of his face, but not seriously wounded. The army was all over the capital city, stopping all cars, looking for evidence of guns or suspicious individuals.

We left the next morning and safely made it out of town, although we were stopped several times. The East Asian people were all stopped and their cars emptied for a very thorough search. When we were stopped we told them that we had been in an accident and were on our way to Nairobi to have the car repaired. With a bent front end and broken headlights the soldiers believed what we said and simply waved us on. When we arrived at the Uganda-Kenya border it was closed. So we found a nice hotel in the town of Tororo.

The next morning we were very grateful the border was open and we reached Nairobi, able to find the Grover home with no difficulty. With Dale's help we got our car into a garage for repairs, two days before Christmas.

The Grover kids and ours hit it off nicely. Opening Christmas gifts was a most delightful time.

Camping on the Indian Ocean

The Grovers had planned to take us on a camping trip to the Indian Ocean, south of Mombasa, over the New Year. Since our car was in the garage we all piled into Dale Grover's VW Kombi, which included nine of them and six of us, along with our tents, camping gear, suitcases, and food. With such a load Dale was only able to average forty miles an hour.

On the way south we arrived on the scene of a horrible accident. A car had tried to pass going up a hill on a two-lane highway, resulting in a head-on collision with another car coming over the hill. The ambulance had already left the scene taking the severely injured people to the hospital. There were seven bodies lying beside the road, four adults and three children, all deceased. I got out of the car and checked all seven of them to be sure there was no life in any of them.

Following that tragic delay we resumed our trip, arriving at the campground eighteen miles south of Mombasa, about 7:45 p.m. The tents went up and we all rolled into our sleeping bags.

The next morning we could appreciate the awesome campsite next to the beautiful white sand of the Indian Ocean. We got our snorkels and enjoyed looking at the beautiful fish out by a nearby reef, as well as digging in the sand. The sun was very hot and Anna, who never got a sunburn because of her beautiful Italian skin, got her first burn. Other missionaries arrived and we all had a great time of fellowship and laughter.

The next night Anna made a huge spaghetti dinner that everybody enjoyed.

We spent five nights and four days frolicking on the beautiful beach and in the lovely ocean. We returned to the Grover home safely on January 2.

Returning home

I contacted the garage and found that they needed another four or five days to complete the repairs. I was disappointed since we were supposed to be back at Ruanguba on January 3. On the other hand, we were delighted to have five more enjoyable days to spend with the Grovers. We left them on Friday, January 9, being quite sad that we had to say goodbye. We arrived home safely three days later to a pile of Christmas mail.

Visiting Mission Hospitals and National Parks

Prince Albert National Park, Congo

In the fall we decided to take a short family trip to an animal park, not too far from Ruanguba. Soon after entering the park, driving on a one-lane dirt road, we came across a large lion walking along the grass next to the road, only ten feet away. What a sight! He didn't pay any attention to us so we got some good pictures. Further along, we came across a large pride of lions with their cubs, with ten or twelve taking turns feeding on one of the park animals. As we slowly drove around the park we saw a variety of other animals.

When we explained to missionary friends back at the station what we saw, one long-term missionary lady was a bit jealous. She'd been to the park several times in the past twenty years but had yet to see one lion.

The next April we took a fifteen-day trip to visit other hospitals and national parks. As we drove through that particular park again we found a good-size pond with a lot of hippos. One of the hippos was off by itself so I started to chase it with our car. Debbie and Becky cried out, "No, Daddy!"

Dan, on the other hand, said, "Faster Daddy!"

Anna just looked at me with disgust. I stopped the chase and we got back on the main road. We soon arrived at the Hurlbert's home in Butembo, where we spent the night.

Nyankunde Mission Station, Congo

The trip to Nyankunde was north and on a very rough and rocky road. It took us into the Ituri Rain Forest. Just inside the rain forest lived a large group of pygmies, their average height about four to five feet. There was a medical clinic there and our nurse, Pat Person, had arranged for me to examine some of the ill pygmies.

While I was doing that Anna was waiting with the children in our station wagon. It was a hot day so the windows were rolled down. Several pygmies gathered around, talking in their native tongue. Anna wanted to have some pictures of them, however, as she started shooting they became very irate at her and began shouting. Surprised and not sure what was happening she had the kids quickly roll up the windows. The pygmies gathered around the car shouting and pounding on it. Soon they were rocking the car, which frightened Anna and the kids a great deal.

Just then Pat and I arrived back at the car after treating some of the sick pygmies. Pat realized what had happened and quickly spoke to them in their own tongue, saying, "*Munganga* (Swahili for Doctor) McQuoid came to your clinic today to examine and give healthcare to your people. So don't frighten or harm his family," which calmed them down. Later we learned the pygmies believed that if someone took their picture they were stealing their soul, so they refused to let anyone take their photo.

Following that interesting and scary experience we continued on the road north through the Ituri Rain Forest. The road was narrow in many places allowing only one vehicle at a time. In addition, there were many mud holes because of the frequent rain. Trucks would pass through and often get stuck, leaving deep ruts. Rocks were often brought in to help fill up the ruts and holes. As long as I kept the wheels out of the ruts I was able to keep the car moving. Fortunately, nothing was coming our way when we arrived at one huge mud hole, stretching about 120 feet in length. This was the biggest challenge we'd ever faced on these horrible African roads and I wondered if we'd be able to make it to the other side.

Asking everyone to pray and driving as fast as I dared over the rocky, muddy road, we made it, with some new dents but otherwise intact station wagon. I can still remember hearing the girls scream as we bounced along. I sincerely believe that our guardian angels were lifting and pushing our vehicle, allowing us to safely reach the other side. We gave thanks and traveled on, arriving at Nyankunde Mission Station a short while later.

Nyankunde was a large station with five different mission organizations working together. The hospital was well-equipped and looked much nicer than ours at Ruanguba. During the five days we stayed there I enjoyed making rounds with Dr. Carl Becker, who was a very intelligent, wise physician.

The station had a nice pool, which the kids really enjoyed. We had a great time meeting new friends. It was wonderful meeting Calvin Smith, a fellow Wheaton College grad, and his family.

Murchison Falls National Park, Uganda

We drove east to our next national park, which was in Uganda. Murchison Falls is the largest and most scenic park in Africa. It was exciting to see many elephants and other wild animals as we drove to Paraa Lodge, where we had a reservation. We arrived on April 11, and that evening we listened to the "Voice of America" radio station and heard the blast-off of Apollo 13.

The following morning we drove around the park, amazed at the beauty of God's creation: the landscape, beautiful trees, wildflowers, birds, and animals, et cetera.

In the afternoon we took a tourist boat trip up the Nile River to the Falls. There were crocodiles and hippos in abundance, some close to our boat. Then we hiked around beautiful Murchison Falls.

The next day my foolish, risk-taking mindset came to the surface. We were going to the Falls via a south bank trail that crossed the Nile River by ferry. On the way we saw a big elephant, forty to fifty feet from the road, walking slowly away from us. Road signs advised tourists to stay in their respective cars at all times. But who wants to take the picture of the backend of an elephant? Not me! So I got out of the car with our camera, proceeded to walk diagonally toward the elephant, trying to snap a side view. Since he was just lazily eating grass as he moseyed along I felt safe. But when I was about thirty feet away he suddenly whirled around with ears extended, head and trunk up. Fortunately, he didn't charge, but I took off for the car with the speed of an ostrich—almost. Reaching the car, I realized the elephant was looking at me, so I took two quick pictures, jumped in the car, and drove off. At least I got a front view of the elephant, though at the risk of having a "cardiac arrest." My family has never let me forget that.

When I got up early on Tuesday, April 14, I was fortunate to see a comet in the sky. I quickly awakened Anna and Danny. We were in awe at the majestic view in the northeastern skies. In the meantime, a mother elephant and her young offspring walked right by our back door.

Later that day we decided to look for rhinos in the park and soon came upon a mother rhino and her offspring facing us, seventy feet off to the side of the road. The narrow one-lane road had a mud hole in it, which I didn't see as I was very intent on watching the rhinos. All of a sudden, to my dismay, I became stuck in this hole, unable to go forward or backward. I panicked, fearful the mother rhino might charge us thinking we were endangering her offspring. I shouted, "Anna and Danny, jump out and push this car while I drive!" They did and we got out of the mud hole, the two rhinos just looking at us, probably thinking, "Those humans are really goofy." That was another act of "heroism" on my part that my family won't let me forget.

Queen Elizabeth National Park, Uganda

The next day proved to be another eventful and scary day. We left the lodge and drove three hundred miles south to the Mweya Lodge, in Queen Elizabeth National Park. The foothills of the Mountains of the Moon, between Congo and Uganda, were beautiful until we ran into clouds and rain. We were surprised there was a section of blacktop to drive on. However, to reach the park and our lodge we had to turn off onto a black dirt road. It had rained quite hard so the surface was as slippery as ice, which I didn't realize. All of a sudden the car slid, turned 180 degrees, then kept sliding backward down the road. Finally we ran off the road into a shallow ditch, the backend going up a three foot embankment and coming to a sudden stop. The carrier on the top of the car flew off and landed right side up. We were grateful that no one was hurt and that the car didn't roll over.

Our guardian angels came to the rescue once again. A "good Samaritan" stopped and took Anna and the girls to the lodge, where they sent back help to get the car back on the road. Thankfully, I was able to drive to the lodge, a couple of miles away. The next day the lodge workshop welded the muffler and replaced the carrier on top of the car.

We spent a couple of days enjoying the large pool, and driving around the park, seeing all kinds of wild animals. Our guide took us to a place in the park where the lions sleep in trees—the most unusual sight we'd ever seen.

On Saturday, April 18, we drove safely back to Ruanguba, very glad to be back at our Congo home.

Climbing Nyriagongo

Climb one

One fall weekend, a few of the mission staff decided to take the older school kids for a climb up Mount Nyriagongo. They invited Anna and me to join them.

The mountain was fifty kilometers southwest of our mission station, located in the Virunga Mountain Range of east-central Congo. It's 11,380 feet high, with a main crater of 1.3 miles wide, and 820 feet deep, containing a liquid lava pool, known for its devastating eruptions. We started the climb carrying lots of water and lunch. We were able to stay with the group in the lower part of the climb, but not when the trail became steep, as we were out of shape and required frequent rest stops. The group arrived at the top and enjoyed spectacular views of the surrounding area and looked inside the volcano with its fiery, bubbling lava far below.

An hour or more later when Anna and I arrived, clouds had moved in, completely enveloping the top of the mountain. We could see nothing but fog all around us. Disappointed, we simply turned around and began our descent, glad it was much easier going down.

Climb two

It was the following May that our fellow missionary Paul Hurlbert and I decided to climb the mountain and spend the night, so took along sleeping bags, food, and lots of water, with a guide and three porters to help carry our stuff. It took four and a half hours from where we'd left our car to climb to the top of the rim, arriving at 2 p.m. Such an amazing sight watching the explosion of boiling lava in the crater below us. As nighttime came we were awestruck at the beauty of the entire sky above the mountain glowing red. Later Anna said that from our yard at Ruanguba she could see the glow.

Paul and I then went an hour's distance down the mountain to what was known as jeet level, where we found protective huts for us to sleep in.

The hike down was a miserable experience as my big toes kept rubbing in my shoes, loosening one of my big toenails. We put our sleeping bags in one of the huts and lit a fire at the entrance and slept reasonably well.

The next morning after breakfast I cut holes in the tip of my shoes to take the pressure off during our descent. That felt a lot better but the shoes were ruined.

Climb three

Shortly after the second climb, some of the staff at the mission station decided to take any interested students to climb the mountain. Anna wanted to climb this time, so we decided to improve our physical condition by jogging two miles most mornings on the mountain road between our house and the hospital. That did help us a great deal when it came time to climb. Danny was excited about joining the climb as well, although he didn't need to get in shape.

There were twenty-four of us on this hike with eighteen porters to carry all the food, tents, and sleeping bags we needed. We had a good climb to the top, although Danny and the other young ones beat us by a good margin. Even though the kids had fun crawling all around the rim of the volcano, I was sad to see that the volcanic activity was much less than what I'd seen three weeks earlier..

The girls slept in one big tent and the guys in smaller tents. Danny and I decided to sleep in the same sleeping bag, lying on a ledge just inside the volcanic edge. I made a mattress of everlasting flowers but that did little to soften the rocks underneath us. Danny had an upset stomach during the night, which added to his discomfort. It ended up being a pretty miserable night.

The next morning started with a clear sky for a short time and then turned cloudy and very cold. After breakfast we packed our stuff and the porters came up from the jeets where they'd spent the night. We took our time going down while Danny ran down nonstop, making him the first one down, taking only an hour and a half to reach the cars.

Where Do We Go from Here?

With the coming of the New Year we began to pray, asking what God had in store for us. Initially there was a possibility of staying a second year, until we heard another physician was planning on coming to Ruanguba this year to join Dr. Cullen. Anna thought that we should resettle in a small town in the States. Feeling very challenged with the medical work at Ruanguba Hospital I wondered if we should consider full time medical missionary work in Congo. However, we agreed that we should return to the States, probably Minnesota, and continue seeking God's direction for our future.

Putting out some feelers

On January 26, I wrote three letters to different Christian clinics in Minnesota. The first one was to Dr. Wally Anderson at the Golden Valley Clinic, the second went to Dr. Ray Magnuson at the Cambridge Clinic, and the third to Dr. Ernie Lorentzen of Detroit

Lakes. I explained that our one year of medical missionary work was coming to an end and I was looking for a medical practice to join for an indefinite period of time. We prayed over those letters, asking for clarity and discernment in this next chapter of our lives, and then mailed them in Kisoro.

Interesting mail

When we returned to Ruanguba after a trip visiting mission hospitals and national parks there was interesting mail awaiting us. One was a letter from Dr. Wally Anderson inviting us to join the Golden Valley Clinic. He said we could come and practice in the group as long as we desired. If and when we sensed God's call to return to the mission field we would be free to go. That was very encouraging to us.

There also was a letter from Dr. Baker of the CBFMS commenting on the mission field and how well he thought we were doing. He encouraged us to prayerfully consider full time mission work. In addition, we received a copy of the *Littlefork Times* newspaper telling of a reception for the new doctor, Dr. Doran, and how patients were being admitted to Littlefork Hospital. That was a clear indication the door to return to the medical practice in Littlefork was closed.

Two days later a letter came from Dr. Ray Magnuson, saying the Cambridge Clinic was interested in my joining, "If I would become a permanent partner."

Dr. Lorentzen's letter of interest never arrived until the end of June, well after we had made our decision.

Decision made

After a lot of prayer we finally made our decision. On April 20, 1970, I wrote in my diary, *"We felt this was the final indication of the Lord's directing us to the Golden Valley Clinic as a place where He wanted us."* Little did we know the significance of this decision and the long-term implication it had for our family. But we were at peace, standing on God's Word: *"For we walk by faith and not by sight"* (2 Corinthians 5:7 NASB).

Once our future was settled, we began to direct our thoughts to what needed to be done for our move back to the US. We made a list of things we wanted to sell, such as our washing machine, freezer, refrigerator, pots and pans, my tools, our Toyota station wagon, the movie and slide projector, and many other things. We also looked to buy some mementos of our year in Congo, such as oil paintings, curios, the skin of a twenty foot python, a zebra skin, an African drum, various pictures of wild animals, and two small elephant tusks we had purchased in one of our travels.

We used a travel agent to arrange our trip back to the US. We planned to stop in Nairobi, Kenya, then Israel, Rome, and southern France to visit our good Wheaton College friends, Phil and Nancy Gegner.

The time seemed to fly by in June, our last month in Congo. There was a lot of packing and shipping things back to my brother, Bill's, home in Bloomington, Minnesota. Missionaries, who were stationed some distance away from Ruanguba, arranged to stop by to say farewell and to thank us for giving a year of our lives to work with them. Many expressed hope we would return.

My daughter Becky and I had some minor injuries near our departure time. On June 18 she was playing at school with friends and ran into a cement post, part of a porch on the school building. She knocked out a tooth and had a green stick fracture of her left wrist. Thankfully, a plaster splint for two weeks was all she needed.

Two days later Anna and I were playing softball at the dorm with the kids. Danny threw the ball and it hit me on the tip of my left fifth finger, dislocating it at the middle joint. I simply popped it back in place, taped it to the fourth finger and kept on playing.

As our departure date of July 3, 1970, approached, we were sad to say goodbye to such wonderful new friends. After family devotions on June 29, Debbie began crying over leaving her friends, especially Judy Camp. We had a nice discussion about the joy of heaven when, at some future date, friendships would be renewed forever, which comforted her somewhat.

We finally said our farewells to the Ruanguba missionaries, African nurses, and workers. We'd sold our Toyota station wagon to one of our missionary friends. Pelley, another missionary, drove us to Goma, where I picked up our airline tickets from our travel agent. The Goma missionaries all gathered at Mel and Mary Lyons for a goodbye supper and wonderful fellowship. We stayed in the guesthouse in Goma for our last night in Congo.

Little did Anna and I know the next year or so of our life was going to be the most difficult and challenging, for us and our family.

7

A Traumatic Return to the USA

Returning to the US to join a Christian clinic connected to a large Metropolitan hospital, stirred up several negative emotions in me: fear, anxiety, and insecurity. This impacted our marriage and brought us to an all-time low.

We boarded our first flight in Goma. When the pilot saw the wrapped elephant tusks I was carrying, he decided the safest place for them was next to him in the cockpit. We flew into Bujumbura, where we took a jet to Nairobi, Kenya. The flight attendants allowed me to put the tusks in the back of the plane for that flight, and we had no trouble finding a safe place for them on the rest of our flights home.

After spending six days in Nairobi, we spent a week touring as much of Israel as possible. That was a challenge with four children but was quite enjoyable. We loved swimming in the Sea of Galilee and the Dead Sea, and appreciated seeing the incredible sites around Jerusalem.

Becky had lost a tooth while still in Africa but never put it under her pillow. And while in Israel, Danny and Deb both lost a tooth on the same day. All three decided to put their tooth under their pillow with a note stating: "I would like an American dollar instead of an Israel pound." They got their wish.

After Israel, we spent two days in Rome, then one week in southern France with our dear Wheaton College friends, Phil and Nancy Gegner.

On July 23 we flew back to the good old USA, landing at Kennedy airport. Anna's parents, her brother Tom and his wife Jane, and Anna's sister, Susan, met us. It felt so good to be back in the US.

Travel and Getting Settled

Time with Anna's family

We enjoyed the week with the Tolenos and their extended family. We played some golf and celebrated Danny's ninth birthday on July 27 at Hidden Lake, Pennsylvania, on the Delaware River. We visited Grace Chapel, Anna's church while growing up, and shared our slides and experiences with them. During the week we came to learn how much Anna's parents, Bill and Marie, disapproved of my "taking Anna and the kids to Congo," the previous year. They thought of Congo like a jungle in a Tarzan movie with roaring lions and had been very concerned for our safety.

Our new transportation

A week later we flew out of LaGuardia Airport, landing in Detroit, where my sister, Jeannie, her husband, Vern, and their kids, Pam and Tim, met us. They drove us to the General Motors auto dealer where we picked up our 1970 Buick LaSabre three-seater station wagon. I had placed an order for this car while we were still in Congo and were thrilled to have such a beautiful, spacious car. We then drove the forty-five miles to Vern and Jeannie's home and spent a delightful weekend with them. On Sunday we were privileged to share some of our experiences in Congo, along with slides, at their church.

Do we have any bugs?

Our next stop took us to Wheaton, Illinois, thirty miles west of Chicago. It was fun showing our kids Wheaton College, the place where we'd met and spent four years of our lives.

However, the next day was not a fun day. We called it "a visit to purgatory." Every missionary family returning to the US was required to go into Mt. Sinai Hospital in Chicago for health testing. Stool and blood samples had to be taken to make sure none of us were carrying any unwanted "bugs." As they wanted good samples each of us had to take a laxative—yuck! Anna had the extra responsibility of helping our three daughters while I only had to deal with our son. The good news was that we all came through with flying colors, even though it wasn't much fun.

Report to Dr. Milton Baker

The mission headquarters for CBFMS was located in Wheaton. We met with Dr. Baker, the Foreign Secretary of the Mission Board for Congo, among other countries. He wanted to hear about our experiences the past year and our plans for the future, while Elfie Pruitt, one of our missionaries from Congo, cared for our children.

As we shared with Dr. Baker it was very clear that we'd been united in our desire the previous year to spend one or two years at Ruanguba, a great experience for all of us. As that year passed, we'd prayed for a clear direction from God on whether he wanted us in full-time medical mission service or for us to return to a medical practice in the States.

But now, sitting in Dr. Baker's office, it was equally clear that we were no longer on the same page regarding God's direction for our future.

During the past year I'd been challenged, yet thoroughly enjoyed the medical work. I leaned toward eventually returning, even though it would require raising financial support, followed by a year or more of language study.

On the other hand, Anna felt strongly against full-time medical mission service because of the impact it would have on our children when they moved into ninth grade. Depending on which mission field we went to, the likelihood was we would have to send them to boarding school for their high school years. If we ended up at Ruanguba, each child would ultimately be sent to a Christian school known as Rift Valley Academy in Central Kenya, at least a two-day trip away. Anna's mother's heart made that decision unthinkable. She quoted a Scripture verse, 1 Timothy 5:8 (NASB), *"But if anyone does not provide for his own, and especially those of his own household, he has denied the faith and is worse than an unbeliever."* In effect, she was clearly stating that no one else would be raising our children because that was our God-given responsibility, not a boarding school's.

As Anna shared her strong feelings, Dr. Baker and I sat in silence for a while. Then Dr. Baker asked a question we'll never forget, "Can't you trust God to care for your children?"

That ended meeting as far as Anna was concerned. She got up and moved to the back of the room in tears. That question was the epitome of spiritual abuse, although I didn't recognize it as such at that time. I continued talking to Dr. Baker for a short while before we left. With such a hurtful ending we were glad to leave his office.

Once outside, Anna stated firmly, "Don't you ever take me back into that office again."

However, the discussion between Anna and myself continued for months.

I want to say at this point how grateful I am for my dear wife's strong stand on behalf of our children. I have told her that many times over the course of our marriage.

I realized much later that my favoring long-term mission work was not God's call on my life. Rather, it came out of my insecurity and sense of inadequacy practicing medicine in a large Metropolitan hospital among many specialists.

Replenishing items sold in Congo

On Wednesday, August 5, we visited with another family recently home from Congo. They told us about the Missionary Equipment Service in Chicago, a store with excellent prices for returning missionaries. We were able to buy pots and pans, dishes, a movie and slide projector, along with many other necessary items. Then we packed for our trip to Minneapolis the next day.

Renting a home and getting settled

Uncle Len and Aunt Eleanor opened their home to us, moving into the basement and giving us their bedroom. Our first evening, Bill and Shirley and their kiddos, Mike, Tami, Angie, and Holly came over. We had a delightful homecoming meal that only a gourmet cook like Eleanor could fix. Len kept us laughing with his jokes.

The following day while our kids were either playing with or at day camp with Bill and Shirley's kids, we went looking for a rental home. It took us three days of searching but we found a lovely five-bedroom home in Excelsior at a reasonable price of $290 per month.

The next day we went to the local elementary school and registered Danny, Debbie, and Becky in their respective classes. Anna was a little concerned over how Debbie would do since she'd been home-schooled last year, but she entered the second grade without difficulty, Danny the fourth, and Becky started kindergarten.

That afternoon I had a meeting at the Golden Valley Clinic where I met my future partners. They were all there except Dr. Wally Anderson who was on his way to Taiwan for six weeks. The other family doctors were Dr. Stan Stone, Dr. Gordon Johnson, Dr. Bradley Johnson, and our general surgeon, Dr. Bill Scott, all Christian. I felt very comfortable with each of them and looked forward to being a partner. The plan was for me to start the first of September.

Our first weekend was spent with my dad and mom at Parkers Prairie, Minnesota. Vern, Jeannie, and their two kiddos were there as well. It was so good to see them. Dad asked us to take over the pulpit and share experiences of the past year, which we were glad to do. During the evening service we showed slides.

Now that we had our house, our next big task was retrieving all the various pieces of furniture stored or loaned out the previous year in Littlefork, International Falls, and Chisholm. After a few phone calls we decided on the best time to make the six-hour trip to northern Minnesota, where we'd been asked to speak and to show some of our slides. We took off, excited to see our friends.

We needed a U-Haul truck and trailer along with our station wagon to get everything loaded from all three places. Sunday was a nice day of rest, with John and Nancy Redmond, our good friends now living in Chisholm. Early the next morning we left for Excelsior and our new home.

Upon our arrival, Bill and Shirley came over and were a great help in unloading and putting items in their proper places. It took a week to get our house organized as we wanted.

The following week I started work, feeling anxious as I thought about what lay ahead for me.

A New Medical Practice and My Struggle

Since my medical training days, along with the seven years in Littlefork, I never saw myself living in a big city and working in a large hospital. But to my wonderment, here I was on the staff of North Memorial Hospital and a partner in a six-physician clinic in Golden Valley, a suburb of Minneapolis, Minnesota. I didn't realize until years later that God had had a plan and desire for my inner healing and over time orchestrated events to cause that to happen.

My first day

September 1 came and I met our surgeon, Dr. Bill Scott, at the hospital. He had a Tuesday morning medical conference known as the Grand Rounds, which included breakfast, and he invited me to join him. Following the conference he had a couple of minor surgical procedures, an inguinal hernia repair and a paracentesis. He invited me to tag along, which I did.

As he did those procedures in a beautiful, modern, and spotless surgical suite I couldn't help but reflect on doing many similar procedures at Ruanguba the previous year. That setting, however, had been poor lighting with minimal equipment and chickens and dogs running around just outside the window of the operating room. Last year it was one other physician and myself doing every possible procedure that presented itself. But at this hospital there was a wide variety of surgical and other medical specialists. I felt like a lonely family physician in a large hospital where I didn't measure up, leaving me quite anxious and fearful.

I made rounds in the hospital with Dr. Scott the rest of the morning, enjoying getting to know him and talking about patients. He and his wife had spent many years on the mission field before joining the Golden Valley Clinic. The afternoon was spent at the clinic seeing patients with Dr. Brad Johnson. I had a full schedule and enjoyed seeing patients, the inner turmoil I was feeling having no impact on my patient care.

My closing note in my diary for this day was, *"I felt like a fish out of water at the hospital and the clinic—everything is so new."* A few days later I recorded another fish comparison in my diary: *"One really feels like a small fish in a big pond. I'm sure the Lord has many lessons to teach me while we are here."*

Surgical privileges

My discomfort for being on the staff of a large hospital was further aggravated when in mid-October I found out I had to write a special letter to the surgical chief of staff at North Memorial Hospital, requesting surgical privileges, for which I would have to show proof of my experience and training. I clearly understood why such a request was made, however, the feeling of inadequacy rose up in me. Once again I wished I could return to the mission field, or at least to a small town where I wouldn't struggle with these emotions.

Weekend yo-yo

The opportunities to leave on occasion to visit my parents made me realize the emotional yo-yo experience I was having by leaving the city on Friday and returning on Sunday. When I left home I had a sense of lightness, joy, and peace—like a bird being let out of a cage to fly. When I returned home I felt anxiety and heaviness return to my soul, as if I were being put back into a cage. This weekend emotional turnaround continued in varying degrees for at least a year or more.

Attempts to change Anna's mind

As time went on I began to adjust to my medical practice and enjoyed the full gamut of family medicine and connection with my patients. I also related well with my partners and employees.

However, in the evenings I frequently talked with Anna about the things we'd done in Congo the previous year, based on my diary. Invariably I would ask the question, "Wouldn't you like to still be there?" Or "Return there?"

She always responded with a strong negative answer, ending our conversation. These repeated talks came to a climax when one evening I told her I felt God really wanted us back on the mission field. She'd had enough of my trying to persuade her to do something she would never do and her answer was powerful, nearly flooring me, but it was just what I needed to hear. "Well, then you just go back to the mission field and I will stay here with the kids."

That statement, in essence, ended the repetitious discussions over returning to a foreign field. There was no way I'd consider leaving my family.

House Hunting

Realizing that my partners liked me and hoped I would remain with them on a long-term basis, we began looking for a house. Our search started mid-February and ended March 25, 1971, when we purchased a five-bedroom house in Golden Valley, at 2155 Cavell Avenue North. We were thrilled over becoming homeowners and it had a settling affect on the whole family. There was a great deal of excitement when we moved into our home mid-June. It was amazing to find a medical school classmate of mine, Irv Katz, and his wife, Karen, living just across the street from us with their three daughters, close in age to our three girls. What an extra blessing that was for us.

We had a true sense that this was our home and we were where God wanted us for this season in our life. We didn't know what lay in store for us down the road, but God did. I find it amazing as I think back on it, how, even though I had a wrong understanding of Him, He still loved me, pursued me, and used me for His glory and my good. One of my favorite Scripture verses is Jeremiah 29:11 (NIV), " 'For I know the plans I have for you,' declares the LORD, 'plans to prosper you and not to harm you, plans to give you hope and a future.' "

Family - 1936

Sandstone, MN - 1940

Tad and Tyke - February 1938

1937 Chev and family - early 1940s

Tess, Tad, and Tyke

Milk source - Alllendale, IL

The terrific trio

Family - 1946

Family - 1948

Dave age 12

On patrol with my best buddy Roland Jordahl

Time to make some money

Palm Sunday - 1950

The McQuoid musicians

Lake Benton High School Quartet

The muscle guys

Family - 1952

My hook shot

My jump shot

Making fudge with help from home economics teacher

Wheaton College tower

High School graduation

Bill and I settling in dorm - Wheaton College

Summer work building silos

Wheaton College graduation picture

Taking Anna to Washington Banquet - February 1957

Our wedding - July 21, 1958

Our parents

Our wedding party

McQuoid family

UNIVERSITY OF MINNESOTA
MEDICAL SCHOOL

Recognition Program
honoring the
Senior Class in Medicine

MAYO MEMORIAL AUDITORIUM
FRIDAY AFTERNOON, JUNE 9, 1961
AT FOUR O'CLOCK

Medical school program

Medical school graduation

Our Littlefork home

Family reunion - August 1968

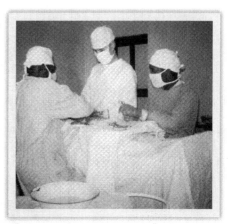

Doing surgery at Ruanguba Mission - Congo, Africa

Family on return from Congo

Girls love their striped pj's

Family - 1976

Surprise 25th wedding anniversary - 1985

Dad's 88th birthday

Debbie and Dave's wedding –
June 15, 1985

Melanie and Craig's wedding –
July 1, 1989

Becky and Dan's wedding — July 26, 1986

Dan and Rose's wedding - September 7, 1991

Matt and Tami's wedding - August 9, 1997

The doc at work

Blue merle collie dog Gypsy

Dr. Bruno receiving my bag

Passing of my doctor's bag

— 8 —

Settling in
and Moving Forward

The steps that followed proved to me that this was the medical practice where God wanted me to be on a long-term basis.

In spite of all the emotional turmoil within myself, my partners never knew what I was going through. They felt I was doing a good job and were quite pleased to have me in the group. I chose not to tell them, being afraid of what they'd think of me. In the middle of January 1971, they made plans to incorporate as a business in July, and said they would like to have me join the group, which was so reassuring to me.

Gradually the thoughts of wanting to return to the mission field faded away as I realized that this is where God had planted me and my family. And I was grateful.

I Can't Believe they Chose Me!

My practice went well that first summer, in spite of my ongoing inner struggles of feeling inadequate. The business meeting to incorporate the clinic didn't take place in July, but was put off until August 2. On that evening, the six doctors, along with our attorney met for the big meeting.

Among the many things that needed discussion was the election of officers for the corporation. There was no talk over who should be in what role, rather, Dr. Wally Anderson promptly nominated me to be the president. And all the other docs unanimously said, "Yes."

I sat there speechless and in shock, thinking, "Why me? I'm not qualified. I've only been here eleven months. This doesn't make sense." But they were lovingly firm about wanting me in that position. So I took over the meeting and ran it the best I could, having no idea I would stay in that position at the clinic until I retired on April 29, 1999.

I did feel more settled in the medical practice after their vote of confidence. On October 18, 1971, I entered in my diary, *"Nice visit with Bill Scott. He complimented me on my consciousness and thoroughness. I appreciated that."*

Church Hunting

We struggled for the first couple of years deciding which church we should attend. While living in our rental home in Excelsior, we initially attended Minnetonka Baptist Church. However, when we moved to our new home in Golden Valley, we began looking for a church closer to home. We were drawn to both Northwest Baptist Church and Crystal Evangelical Free Church, which quite upset Dad and Mom. I wrote in my diary July 22, 1971, *"Letter from Dad was quite upsetting to us. He and Mom are unhappy that we aren't choosing to go to a conservative Baptist church."* I responded only in my diary, *"So narrow-minded."* Dad always felt that the CB church was doctrinally correct compared to any other Baptist or Evangelical church.

One key factor that helped us spiritually, as well as settled the church decision for us, was being introduced to the Lay Evangelism Outreach (LEO) program at Crystal Free. Pastor Tom McDill was key in bringing this to the church, and we decided to be a part of that new ministry.

We'd always felt very inadequate over making a clear and concise presentation of the gospel to friends or strangers. That all changed when we embraced this program and learned how to share our faith. We were filled with excitement and joy as we shared the gospel and saw people put their trust in Christ. I soon began sharing my faith with patients, when appropriate, and saw several pray in the office to receive Christ. In time we became leaders in the program, which further gave us the sense that we were where God wanted us.

Medical Practice Changes with New Opportunities

During the late 1970s and early 1980s, significant changes occurred within our clinic. Two family docs left; one retired and one relocated. Our surgeon and his wife felt God's call to return to the mission field. Another family doctor joined us, Dr. Steve Carlson. We had two offices for years in our practice, but now we had to downsize with only four family physicians. We were able to sell the Camden building in North Minneapolis and consolidate everything into the Golden Valley Clinic.

Since we were all interested in medical missions, as we restructured our practice we agreed to set aside a fixed amount of dollars to send one of us on a short-term mission every year. My partners suggested that I be the first to go.

Becky

So on Saturday, February 6, 1982, I took our third child, Becky, a junior in high school, to Honduras for two weeks. We went with the Medical Group Mission (MGM) of the Christian Medical and Dental Association. Our two older children were out of the nest in college and nursing school so were unable to go. It was a great experience for both Becky and me.

I had an "absent-minded professor experience" early in the trip that brought some laughs. We flew into Tegucigalpa, the capital, and stayed at a Bible school residence partway up the mountainside. Sunday was given to organization of different teams to go to various places in Honduras. Our team was assigned to the southern part of that country in the city of Choluteca.

Monday morning we were up early, had breakfast, and started loading the vans. I thought there was ample time to stroll around the Bible school grounds to look at the beautiful orchids, so I did. When I returned to the site where the vans were parked, after only being gone for five short minutes, they were all gone and I was stranded with no ride. One of the missionaries gave me a ride down to the bus depot and instructed me what to say to the taxicab driver in Spanish once I arrived in Choluteca. It was a three-hour, standing room only, bus ride with no one speaking English.

At Choluteca I was able to successfully communicate to the taxicab driver to take me to the Hotel Pacifica. When I walked into the compound by the hotel I saw Becky and our team just milling around. I walked up to her, surprised she wasn't concerned about where I'd been—she hadn't even known I wasn't in any of the vans. It was funny to see the expression on her face as I told her what her absent-minded father had just done.

Melanie

It was four years later that I took Melanie to the Dominican Republic for a two-week MGM mission trip. I was careful not to miss any rides this time. But we had something else happen out of the ordinary. Since Melanie had her mom's Italian black hair and dark skin, she looked very similar to the Hispanic people we were treating at various clinics. Melanie's job at each clinic was to be out front registering patients and checking blood pressures while I was inside with the other doctors, examining patients.

Midway through the first week I was interrupted by one of the interpreters. She told me, with a twinkle in her eye, there was a Hispanic man outside who had been observing Melanie and wanted to make me an offer of a cow in exchange for my daughter. He wanted to give her to his son for a wife. I had no problem in turning that offer down, but we've had a lot of laughs about that over the years.

Matt

In the fall of 1988, Matt and I joined Anna in attending Church of the Open Door at Robbinsdale Auditorium. Matt was thirteen when we switched churches and found it hard to make the transition to fitting into their youth group.

When 1990 rolled around it was my turn to go on another mission trip. This time it was Matt's turn and I could also take Anna with me. The question was, where should the three of us go?

Steve Hanson was the youth pastor at Open Door. He had connected with Pastor Diogene Pierre from Haiti, and taken some youth trips to his village in previous years. I learned he was planning to take a group of young people again in June of this year. So I asked him if Anna and I could go along and have a medical clinic for the people of Tricotte and surrounding villages, while Matt would be involved in whatever the guys were doing in that trip. Steve was excited to have us come along.

I worked hard at getting a good supply of various meds from drug representatives who visited the clinic. I sterilized all the instruments and packed them, along with other necessary items, into several boxes.

We flew into Port-au-Prince, Haiti's capital, on June 13. Upon arrival, we loaded luggage, boxes, and people into the back of two trucks for the trip north. Heavy rains struck but we kept partially dry with a large tarp on each truck.

The gals were dropped off in the village of St. Marc where they were going to conduct Vacation Bible School classes. The rest of us went the full five-hour drive to Tricotte. The guys were put to work finishing up a medical clinic, while Anna and I set up a clinic in the church. She was my pharmacist and helper and Pastor Dio was my interpreter.

The clinic was open six of the twelve days we were there and closed on weekends and times when Dio had to be elsewhere. The people were so grateful for what medical care we were able to give them that we saw over 330 patients in those six days.

Church Responsibilities

The opportunity to serve in any church is always there, and so it was with our church, Crystal Evangelical Free Church. I became involved in different avenues of service at various times but I always was doing something such as the following:

Harvest Crew

Our youth pastor, Keith Krueger, brought the vision of the LEO program to the high school level. He asked if I would help him develop what became known as, "The Harvest Crew." This started in January 1978, and as a twosome, we worked well together because Keith was a visionary and I was a nuts and bolts guy. For the next five years I enjoyed helping train young people in this program, which included our three older children, Dan, Debbie, and Becky. It was a joy to see these young people learn to share their faith and lead others to Christ.

Pastoral call committees

On February 8, 1983, another opportunity to serve came my way, something I didn't ask for and could have turned down but didn't. This one fed my ego, which made it harder to say no. The church wanted to add an associate pastor to our staff to assist our senior pastor. At the annual church meeting a call committee was elected and I was among the ones chosen, and at the first meeting

I was elected chairman, which meant I had the privilege of doing the bulk of the work.

Two years later the same scenario was repeated, following the resignation of our senior pastor. Another call committee was chosen and you-know-who was on it and again got the chairman's job.

Boys Brigade

I left the Harvest Crew responsibilities in January of 1983 to become a part of the Boys Brigade program. Our youngest son, Matt, turned eight in March and this gave me the opportunity to do something with him. A year later, I was challenged to take a leadership role by Pastor Dan Bower, who overlooked the program. After praying about it for a week, I said agreed. By fall, I was the Chief Ranger and overall leader of the entire Brigade program.

I enjoyed the role but often put in hours and hours of preparation because of my perfectionistic mindset. This is revealed in a diary entry of September 14, 1985, "... *worked on Boys Brigade with Stan Erickson ... I'm a little frustrated with all the church work (call committee; B.B.)—unable to spend time with family.*" That made me sound like my dad, putting ministry before family.

I did enjoy doing the program with Matt, especially when in one year, the derby car he made not only won the trophy for the fastest car, but also the trophy for the best one made. The judges had no idea who the owner of each car was until after the events were complete so it was all legitimate. But my fellow Rangers, jokingly, accused me of having something to do with the outcome.

Discovery II class

During the Harvest Crew/Boys Brigade years, '78–'87, I also taught a Sunday school class known as Discovery II. This was a class designed to help "thirsty" people go deeper in their personal walk with God. What a joy to see many grow in their faith, although I spent a lot of time in preparation for each class.

Unfortunately, neither Anna nor I knew how to refuse when requested to do something in the church. We'd simply agree and push harder to try and accomplish whatever was asked.

Speaking for myself, I had the attitude that Dad demonstrated in his ministry, which was, "God's work comes first, even before family." What I didn't realize at that time, was that sometimes what one calls "God's work" may not be His at all. But I didn't learn that until later in life.

However, this set the stage for what was to happen in my medical practice that would truly devastate me, yet proved to be God's pruning work in my life. In John 15:1–2 (NASB, underlining mine), Jesus said, *"I am the true vine, and My Father is the vine-dresser. Every branch in Me that does not bear fruit, He takes away; and every branch that bears fruit, He* prunes *it, that it may bear more fruit."*

$\Longrightarrow$ 9 $\Longleftarrow$

The Crash of 1987

It's amazing how life can go on rather peacefully and serenely for quite some time. Then all of a sudden, a major interruption occurs and one's whole world is turned upside down. So it was with me in the latter part of 1984. An event happened in my medical practice, which took a little over two years for it to resurface. When it reappeared I was sent into an emotional tailspin. However, this turned out to be God's instrument of pruning in my life.

This started with my failure to make a timely diagnosis in an infant patient of mine, resulting in necessary major corrective surgery. Though a specialist said it was a difficult diagnosis to make, I still blamed myself.

A New Patient

A Christian couple brought in their two- or three-month-old baby girl asking me to provide well-baby care for her. They chose me as the doctor because the mother's parents were long-term missionaries and friends of my parents.

The infant was born with a fairly serious blood problem, which required careful following by a pediatric blood specialist. But the parents wanted me to do the well-baby checkups, including giving the appropriate immunizations. I was pleased to do that and carefully documented my examinations in her chart, including what I thought to be "normal hip joint development."

Shortly after the child's one-year birth exam the grandmother returned with the girl and her parents, saying, "I think there's something wrong with my granddaughter's hips."

I reexamined her hips and took X-rays, which to my shock and despair, showed bilateral congenital hips. This is a condition, which, if discovered in the early months of a baby's life, can be treated easily by splinting her hips. However, since undiscovered until nearly thirteen months of age, surgery was required to correct the dislocations.

Needless to say, I was distraught over my failure to make the diagnosis in the early months of the infant's life. In tears I apologized to the parents, expressing my deep sorrow. They gave me an abundance of grace by forgiving me and holding no bitterness toward me. Understandably so, the parents chose to take their daughter to another physician for ongoing well-child care. This discovery occurred in November of 1984, but remained dormant until January of 1987. The initial emotions I had became buried in the ongoing business of my medical practice.

Seeking Financial Help

In the first part of January 1987 the parents came to see me because of the significant cost for the two surgeries that had been done. The father was a self-employed painter without any insurance and a family with four older children. They wondered if my malpractice insurance could be used to pay for the expenses. The father's brother was an attorney who was encouraging them to file a malpractice suit. Because of the parents' Christian belief they didn't feel it was right to bring a lawsuit against a fellow believer.

I contacted my malpractice insurance, but they stated that the parents would need to file a lawsuit against me and let the court decide.

At that time, there was a Christian Conciliation Services (CCS) operational in the Twin Cities. This organization worked with disputes of any kind between Christians so lawsuits could be avoided. I arranged to go to the parents' home to talk with them about this organization, not knowing if there would be any financial outcome for them. They were willing, so a meeting was arranged on January 27, 1987.

Besides the presence of the parents and myself, were an attorney representing my malpractice insurance, a family physician, an orthopedic surgeon, and a representative from CCS. There was open discussion about the case, the impact on the child and her parents, and her current status.

The orthopedic surgeon made it clear that it was very difficult to diagnose bilateral congenital hips in the early months of life because they were symmetrical and seemed to have a good range of motion. It's much easier to diagnose a congenital hip, when present in just one hip. I once again asked if my malpractice insurance could help out financially in some way. The attorney's response was the same.

Looking at my missed diagnosis and the effects it had on the child as well as her parents really tore me up emotionally. It triggered a lot of shame and negative thoughts about myself as a person and as a physician. I couldn't forgive myself for missing that diagnosis even though her parents, my partners, the orthopedic surgeon, and others could and did forgive me. I struggled with the question, "Why can't I minister grace to myself when others, especially the parents, minister grace to me?" I felt there were some deeper issues within me that needed to be looked at and resolved. I was broken but didn't know where to turn.

It was just at this time that I received a phone call from a Christian therapist whom I'd never met, calling because one of his clients was a good friend of mine and so wanted to meet me. He thought I might be able to send new clients his way. I believe God orchestrated the phone call while I was hurting emotionally, wanting help without knowing where to turn. We met for lunch and I ended up sharing some of my story with him, resulting in becoming one of his clients.

Thus began a journey for the next four years, of self-discovery and inner healing, aided by a variety of resources, but all directed by the Holy Spirit.

⤗ 10 ⤖

Meeting the God of Grace

My search began with stopping all religious activity I'd been doing to make myself look good on the outside and to feel connected to God on the inside. I sought help from a variety of sources, including Christian counseling, appropriate books, and conferences. Switching to our present church was also helpful. Each of these played a significant role in my inner healing. After searching for four years, I realized I had been following the wrong god all of my life. That is when I met the God of Grace and was forever changed!

was born at home on Sunday, September 13, 1936. At the time, Dad was pastoring three small churches in an area surrounding Lake Nebagamon, Wisconsin.

The atmosphere and teaching of my parents, gave me a desire for a relationship with Jesus, not knowing what that really meant. Dad recorded in his five-year diary on February 5, 1941, *"Tad asked Jesus to come into his heart at nap time."* I was four and a half years of age. He said nothing more about that experience in his diary, but I remember it as a significant decision for me.

I remember events in my growing up years, whether it was at a Bible camp or some special meeting at our church, where I recommitted my life in a desire to walk closer to God. I believe such events indicated that I had a heart for Him but struggled to walk in a way that I thought would be pleasing to my heavenly Father. My faith was strengthened when I went to Wheaton College where I sat under many godly professors and heard great speakers talking about a deeper walk with God.

During the ensuing years, I was sincere in my faith, desiring to know God more intimately. However, I felt I didn't measure up to the standards I thought He had for me. I tried working harder at my faith but always fell short. I wondered if He really loved me as I felt so distant from Him. More effort exerted in "spiritual activity" didn't seem to bring me any closer to God. This struggle continued through the first fifty-four years of my life.

The Onion Begins to Peel

Little by little, with the help of my therapist, I began to learn about my dysfunctional behavior and how it had developed in me. It was a slow, painful process, but one that began opening my eyes of understanding.

Shame and performance

I first learned about shame and the negative effect it had on me in my therapist's office. When I did or said something triggering my shame I would immediately have negative thoughts such as, "I'm no good," "I'm worthless," "I'm a lousy dad," and, "I've got to try harder." Depending on which event brought on those thoughts and feelings they would remain with me, sometimes for days. I ruminated on them until something changed my thought-life.

I also realized I was very performance-oriented, always having to perform well, be it in school, sports, or any activity, and later as a physician, in order to feel accepted.

This mindset made me try very hard to win God's approval but I never felt I got it. The result of all of this was that I grew up feeling very insecure about myself, inadequate, and inferior to most people. I was plagued with the "fear of man." Although this didn't include my patients or friends that I got to know quite well, it did include most people that I met on a social basis. I was able to cover up all those feelings and look good on the outside so no one had a clue what I was feeling on the inside.

Unwritten rules

I learned from my therapist that there were unwritten rules in many families, and certainly there were in ours. One such law was the "do not talk" rule over things that are really important, such as how I really feel or what bothers me. Whenever they were having problems in ministry or other things in their lives, Dad always told Mom, "Don't listen to your feelings. Give them to God." In essence, he was saying to deny any feelings of sadness, hopelessness, anger, frustration, depression, anxiety, fear, or other similar emotions. So I learned to bury my feelings deep inside.

What I missed from Dad

One of the things that stands out in my mind was a statement I heard my mom say frequently, "We have to be an asset to Dad's ministry." I didn't understand the true meaning of what she said until I was in recovery of family of origin issues, meaning that issues from previous generations are passed down to children, such as anger, addiction, control, et cetera. Then I realized it meant "God's work" came before family or anything else.

I know Dad loved me but he didn't show it by spending time with me or teaching me how to do things or make repairs around the house. Dad was a great handyman having grown up in the Great Depression, and knew how to make things last. But he never realized how important it was for him to take me under his wing and teach me what he knew. I needed to be nurtured by my dad in a far deeper way by his being present to me.

What I truly wanted is expressed in a book written by Steve

Farrar titled *King Me**. The book clearly points out how a young son desires to be mentored by his dad. One quote from his book expressed well what I so strongly needed from my dad: "*You've got to purposefully design a time of quiet where you can hear the inside of your son's heart.*" Oh how I wish now that Dad had understood how important it was for him to make time to listen to my heart.

My inner turmoil

As I began to understand these things I initially felt like I was being torn apart, weeping off and on for months. My therapist said, "You're an iceberg starting to melt, but there is a lot more beneath the waterline."

Once I realized how much I was trying to perform in order to get close to God, I stopped doing "religious activity," such as Bible reading and study, praying, tithing, and even church attendance on occasion. I felt like a ship out to sea without a rudder. I couldn't rely on past "religious activities" to connect me with God. Yet somehow I knew God was at work, although I didn't know where He was or what He was doing.

Switching to Another Church

Later I realized God was redirecting us to a different church and He used my dear wife to lead the way.

Anna had become worn out with too many commitments and decided to stop some of her ministry activities. But people wouldn't let her rest, constantly asking, "What are you doing now?" A dear friend of hers had previously left the same church and started going to Church of the Open Door. She invited Anna to join her.

Initially that upset me because of my control issues, but I could see that she was deeply impacted by what she was hearing and seeing. I stayed at our church, in part, because I was still leading the Boys

---

* Steve Farrar, *King Me* (Chicago: Moody Publishers, 2005), 87.

Brigade ministry that Matt was involved in. But in the fall of 1988, Matt and I joined her at Open Door. I resigned from the Brigade ministry effective January 1989. What a relief having no church responsibilities.

I was deeply impacted, as was Anna, with the praise and preaching at this new church. I wept through most of the service because I'd never experienced such worship in the past. It was life-giving to hear from the pulpit that I was God's beloved and He loved me just as I was. I didn't have to perform to meet His approval. Initially it seemed too good to be true that such grace abounded just for me—it was hard to take that in. I soon realized that my dad could preach grace for salvation but he'd never understood grace for daily living.

The Pain of Realizing Ministry Came First

The understanding that Dad's ministry was first, before me, came in the middle of a conference my wife and I attended in September 1989 entitled "Breaking the Silence." The speaker, Jeff Van Vonderen, was on the pastoral staff at Open Door. My birthday happened to arrive on a day in the middle of the conference, and I received birthday card from my dad. In it he copied the entry he had put in his five-year diary on the day of my birth, which was on a Sunday.

Dad had been scheduled to speak at two different churches in the morning. The first part of the entry was, "*Sunday, September 13, 1936, cloudy—cool. I got breakfast—got the nurse—Dr. Wilcox at 11:00 a.m.! 12:25 p.m., David Wentworth born.*" (I was born at home.) After the entry he editorialized and wrote in the birthday card, "*I was pastoring three churches then so when you chose to come into the family you made the day and date a little bit difficult for your dad! (Chuckle.)*" He meant what he wrote as a joke, but it felt to me like his preaching ministry was more important to him than my birth. It was like an arrow going deep into my soul. I wept for days over the intensity of the pain I felt.

Forgiveness

I went for a period of time, perhaps a year or so, feeling anger and estrangement from my dad. Mom had passed away several years earlier and Dad had remarried and was living in Long Prairie, Minnesota. As time passed and I was feeling more inner healing I wanted to reconnect with Dad and break our estrangement. I wasn't quite sure how to do it so I prayed for insight and wisdom. Finally I decided to drive up and see him.

As I was driving I had a revelation, or insight, that blew me away. I suddenly realized that Dad had not received from his dad all that he needed and was a wounded man himself. I always knew he loved me, but now I knew he'd done the best he could. That knowledge impacted me to the depth of my soul. I began weeping so much I had to pull over to the side of the road. I felt a flood of forgiveness enter my soul toward Dad. All the negative thoughts and feelings left and I was filled with gratefulness for him. The result being that we had a wonderful visit and I was able to tell him how much I loved him and appreciated him. Our relationship was restored.

Did God Dance for Me?

Lifeworks Clinic

Another event occurred in February 1991 that was significant. I attended a Lifeworks Clinic on January 30 through February 3. It was a conference with teaching and then breaking into small groups to deal with family of origin issues. The small group I was in became quiet close as we shared deeply about our past. One of the new friends I met there was Suzanne Fry. She was touched by some of the things I said and I was impressed with her background as well. After the conference she wrote me a note and referred to a poem that had impacted her. She did not have the lines of the poem but just the main message. It was about God dancing the day I was born.

That spoke to me deeply because my perception had been that dad did not "dance" for me at my birth. Then I questioned, "Did God dance for me at my birth?" Somehow in my head I thought He did, but I just didn't feel it in my heart.

A close friend

A couple of months passed and I was still thinking, "Did God dance for me at my birth?" I met with a close friend of mine with whom I have a deep respect. He knew of the journey that I was on. I shared the poem with him and that I wasn't sure if God had danced for me.

My friend shared some of his earlier life and how his concept of God had been all mixed up with his dad. He felt that his dad was a distant, stern, and hard-to-please individual. He had attributed those same attributes to the god he followed. Then he learned that the true God was not like his father at all, but loved him deeply, passionately, and unconditionally.

As he shared his journey I felt that I was struggling with the same thing. I realized I had attributed some of the negative characteristics of my dad onto God. I had a profound insight for the first time that I'd been following the wrong god all of my life, that the true God was not like some of the negative things I saw in my dad.

A wondering

Later that same day I met with my therapist. I shared with him the above insight and said that I felt like I'd been an idol worshiper all my life—worshiping the wrong god. He then asked me, "What did they do in the Old Testament with idols?"

My response, "They burned them. Does that mean I should burn my Bible?"

He wisely said, "No, I'm not suggesting that you should do that." But it left me wondering.

Dad had the discipline to read the Old Testament once and the

New Testament twice every year. He'd done that for well over fifty years. He referred to this from the pulpit, encouraging others to do the same. It seemed to me that Scripture symbolized "Dad's Book," which led to a legalistic and performance-oriented mindset. That led me to follow the wrong God—at least that was my perception.

My Bibles

It was two days later on Saturday, April 13, 1991, that I awoke at 5 a.m. with a strong sense of wanting to rid myself of the god I had been following for fifty-four years of my life. I wrote a letter to the god of my dad, renouncing him as my god, stating, "I will not follow you any longer!" It was my perception that his god was very distant, harsh, difficult to please, and without unconditional love.

I started a fire in our fireplace, took my two Bibles and slowly tore out the pages. I threw them into the flames, weeping intensely as I did it. I then threw the letter into the flames as well. I sat in front of the fire, continuing to weep for quite some time. (*I find myself nearly weeping again as I write and relive that experience.*) I sensed in my spirit that something very significant had happened and I was grateful.

Later in the morning I shared with Anna and Matt what I had done, and they warmly hugged and affirmed me. My daughter Becky, and her husband, who lived nearby, came over later in the day to rejoice with me. My other three children, Dan, Debbie, and Melanie lived quite far away but I reached them by phone, and they likewise affirmed and rejoiced with me.

Meeting the God of Grace

That evening we went to our Saturday church service. I'd never gone to the altar before but something Pastor Dave Johnson said at the end of his message, stirred me to go forward for prayer. I briefly shared with the gentlemen at the altar what I had done and that my desire was to connect with the true God. As they prayed for me I felt peace and joy come over me. Something wonderful was happening. What I knew in my head moved down into my heart and I met the God of Grace. The One I had been looking for so diligently, wrapped His arms around me and assured me that He "danced for me," not only at my birth but every day of my life. It was a profound and deep experience that's hard to put into words. I felt His unconditional love for me and I know there was rejoicing in heaven because I felt like I had come home. Surprisingly, I didn't have tears or a sense of excitement, just a calm, inner peace that "all was well with my soul."

What Followed

Purchasing a new Bible

For a while I had no desire to purchase another Bible and wondered when I would do so. It was like I needed time to let my recovery from my idolatry to sink in. About a month or so passed and I began to feel a desire for God's love letters to me. I went to a Christian bookstore and asked them to show me some of their Bibles. They had several, but all of them had commentaries explaining what a given passage was all about. I found myself feeling somewhat nauseated as I looked through those Bibles. I only wanted God's Word. I did not want another man's explanation of what he thought the passage meant. So I went to a B. Dalton Bookstore and purchased a "pure" Bible without commentaries. That's the Bible I still use today.

Men's retreat

It was in May 17–19 of the same year that Open Door had a men's retreat. The leader, Dave Nelson, a good friend of mine, knew of my experience with God and asked if I would be willing to share my story in the Friday evening meeting. I agreed, knowing I would need the Holy Spirit to empower me, which is what happened and many men were touched. I shared my story with some tears but without any sense of trying to perform. One man in particular, Nate Pelto, was touched.

Nate had a similar story with a different outcome, but still one that drew him close to God. I didn't realize that Nate was on the schedule for Saturday night's program. I happened to be sitting in the front row for that service when he shared his story of coming to a life in Christ. In his journey he came to enjoy worshiping by dancing to songs that had a special meaning for him. That evening he danced to three songs. He paused before the second song and said, "I deeply appreciated Dave's story last night. I want to dedicate this song to him." He danced to the song "Always There," written and sung by Don Francisco. That was incredibly touching because symbolically there was God dancing and rejoicing over me. I wept for joy.

The next morning the retreat came to an end with a communion service and sharing. I was in touch with sadness, wishing I had met the God of Grace many years earlier. I knew I had wounded my children by following a false god. But a friend said he felt like he had a word for me. It was a verse from Joel, 2:25a (NASB), *"Then I will make up to you for the years that the swarming locust has eaten."* That indeed comforted me and I have lived to see healing and restoration in our family.

Now many years later, the awareness that this God of Grace walks with me remains a solid reality. I know that I am His beloved and that He continues to love me passionately and unconditionally. I do not need to perform to gain His approval. My name is engraved on the palm of His hand. His smile is toward me and His ear is open to my cry.

I'm so grateful for my dad and mom and their love for me. Yes, I was wounded by them, especially Dad, but they were wounded themselves and they did the best they could. I've taken all these wounds to the cross and forgiven them, all the pain of them totally gone. As with any physical wound there's a scar, so too for emotional wounds, but these are scars of beauty because of His wonderful grace poured out on me.

As I have forgiven my parents, I needed to ask forgiveness from my children. I hurt them as a wounded dad, and they have graciously forgiven me. Life becomes so much richer as I continue to walk in forgiveness.

One of my favorite Scripture passages is: Isaiah 53:4–5 (MSG), *"But the fact is, it was our pains he carried— our disfigurements, all the things wrong with us. We thought he brought it on himself, that God was punishing him for his failures. But it was our sins that did that to him, that ripped and tore and crushed him—our sins! He took the punishment, and that made us whole. Through his bruises we get healed."*

My journey did not end there but continues on with a greater degree of wholeness. Life is so much deeper and intimate as I realize that the God of Grace walks beside me and is in me. I also know that the Holy Spirit will be doing more pruning in my life. I know what Jesus told His disciples is true in John 15:1–2 (NASB), *"I am the true vine, and My Father is the vinedresser. Every branch in Me that does not bear fruit, He takes away; and every branch that bears fruit, He prunes it that it may bear more fruit."* Since that day there has been and will continue to be an ongoing pruning in my life.

All of this helped prepare me for a new challenge that happened in my medical practice. I was so glad He was with me on this journey.

A Physician's Nightmare

I thoroughly enjoyed the practice of medicine even though I knew full well I could never please everyone. So it was that I took care of a sixty-five-year-old gentleman on two different office visits. Though I carefully questioned and looked for any heart problems, he remained in denial regarding very significant symptoms with his heart. The end result was a heart attack that took his life. His wife filed a lawsuit against me that lasted for eighteen months and finally went to trial. The emotional trauma of that experience was very difficult, to say the least.

t was noon, Tuesday, August 19, 1997, when my office administrator of the Golden Valley Clinic called me into the new patient registration office. There awaited a young man who turned out to be a courier for a downtown law office. He had a rather unpleasant demeanor as he asked if I was Dr. McQuoid. When I responded in the affirmative, he coldly requested my signature in receipt of a large envelope. As I took the envelope, noting it was from an attorney's office, I felt a chill go down my spine. I knew the contents did not bear good news.

Opening the Mail

I walked down the hall with my administrator and entered her office. As I closed the door, I said to her, "This can't be good!"

The envelope contained a summons from the Fourth Judicial District Court of Hennepin County to give answer to a complaint brought by the wife of one of my deceased patients. It was a four-page document written by her attorney claiming medical negligence in caring for her husband, whom I treated on two occasions at the clinic—April 17, 1996, and July 17, 1996. The document accused me of "incorrect diagnosis, failure to provide a proper thorough medical examination, failure to refer for proper cardiac care, failure to order correct medication and follow-up treatment." The result being he passed away on August 21, 1996.

As I read the summons I felt like I had just been struck with a twenty-pound ball in the pit of my stomach. I recalled the patient well even though those events were over a year old. The first visit was because of a few brief heart palpitations during the previous night. I took a thorough cardiac history, a careful physical, and did appropriate tests, all leading to a normal exam. The second visit was for mild, left shoulder pain that presented like a bursitis. He denied all cardiac symptoms. Shoulder X-rays were negative and I prescribed a medication.

That evening he developed a crushing chest pain and was taken by ambulance to the hospital where he was diagnosed with acute myocardial infarction (heart attack). He underwent coronary artery bypass surgery but had one complication after another that led to his demise thirty-five days later.

It was very difficult for me to see patients the rest of the afternoon. The words in that summons—"negligence, incorrect diagnosis, failure," kept rolling around in my head and heart. They were like swords piercing my innermost being. When I shared the experience that evening with my wife she loudly said, "Those are lies! Don't believe them."

In my head I knew they were lies, but in my heart I felt crushed and wondered if there was some truth in the accusations. That night and for several nights I slept very poorly.

The Waiting Period

The truth of the statement "No man is an island unto himself," became a reality to me over the next eighteen months. It was because of the incredible support I received from my wife, family, many friends, and the Risk Management Team of Health System Minnesota (HSM) that I was able to weather the storm of accusations that came from the plaintiff's attorney throughout the whole process.

In addition to the external accusations were the inner doubts and questions that kept surfacing, "Should I have done something differently?" "Could I have been more thorough, ordered more tests, et cetera?" Even though I knew I treated the patient appropriately for the history he'd given me and the physical findings I'd detected, inner doubts would come at times like arrows deep into my soul.

The worst experience came when my attorney asked me for the names of several family physician colleagues. She wanted to have one of them serve as an expert witness on my behalf. One individual refused because, after reading about the case, he felt he couldn't support me, thinking that I should have done further testing. That was the biggest blow of all and hooked my shame to the point of wondering, "Maybe I was incompetent." This occurred three months after the summons.

At this point, I sought a therapist because of the emotional tailspin I was in. He greatly assisted me in seeing my true value as well as a pocket of shame from which I needed further healing. Many Scripture verses became a source of strength to me, but one especially stood out. It was Romans 8:28, (NASB), *"And we know that God causes all things to work together for good to those who love God, to those who are called according to His purpose."* This also helped me to try and see things from the perspective of the plaintiff. She was probably stuck in her grief over losing her husband and felt justified in taking it out on me. Rather than feeling anger toward her I felt compassion and often found myself praying for her.

One of the frustrating aspects of a lawsuit is the length of time it takes to have it resolved. Mine took one and a half years. Many days I wouldn't think about it at all but it was always there, just under the surface, and would easily come into my conscious mind. Every letter or phone call from the attorney would renew some of those anxious feelings.

Early on I had to respond to twenty-two interrogatives about myself and my practice, i.e., "List all the publishers of medical textbooks you have read in the last five years. And list all the medical journals to which you subscribe."

The next step was to prepare for a deposition scheduled for April of 1998 where the plaintiff's attorney asked me all types of questions in the presence of my attorney. I met with my lawyer for three hours the day before to practice answering possible questions the plaintiff's might ask. Then the morning it was to occur, they postponed the first deposition for a month. Emotionally that was quite a letdown.

By August, the Hennepin County judge who had been assigned to the lawsuit called both parties together to see if there was a possibility of resolving the issue without a trial. I was praying for such a resolution so this suit could be put behind me. However, the plaintiff's demands were so high and unreasonable from our perspective that the judge, after listening to both sides, simply scheduled a trial for February 1, 1999. That meant six more months of waiting for resolution.

I was able to put the trial on the backburner of my life for that time, which helped keep me at peace. Anna and I had planned a celebration of our fortieth wedding anniversary for the latter part of January. It had been on the calendar before the lawsuit was served. The trip was a good thing because we had a wonderful two weeks on St. Thomas Island, returning refreshed and ready to face the trial.

The Trial

I had one week to return to my practice and make final preparations. Time was spent studying, updating family and friends, meeting with my attorney, and praying. The trial started on Monday. On that morning and each morning thereafter, as we drove to the county courthouse we put on a worship tape from Open Door. Singing brought peace and joy as we focused on God, knowing that He was with us in this experience.

The first day we drove to our attorney's office and received final instructions. We proceeded to the courtroom where the plaintiff's family and her lawyer tried to get her to settle out of court. They felt their case was very weak and so wanted to get a little money, if at all possible. The figure of twenty-five thousand dollars was suggested as a possible settlement.

Asked if I would agree to that, I said I probably would, just to be done with the emotional stress I was feeling. I appreciated the support of my wife and my attorney at this point because they said, "You are not guilty! Don't settle." However, the plaintiff absolutely refused any settlement and wanted the trial.

The trial proceeded to jury selection, opening statements, plaintiff's arguments, followed by cross examinations. The plaintiff told how her husband frequently had chest pain and worried about his heart during the months before his first visit to me in my office. I was shocked to hear that because he had denied such symptoms to me. It came to light that the deceased applied for life insurance two months after his first visit to me. In his application he denied any symptoms of chest pain. My attorney, in the cross examination, asked the plaintiff why she thought her husband hadn't told the truth in his application.

Her response, recorded in my journal, was, "Wouldn't you lie when filling out a form for life insurance?"

The trial went on with several other people for the plaintiff. Finally on Thursday, my attorney was able to put my expert witness on the stand, followed by myself, in the afternoon. I was nervous but able to articulate my position well.

Closing arguments came on Friday. The plaintiff's lawyer compared me to a truck driver with a flawless record, who one day was inattentive, ran a red light, struck a car, and killed someone. That hurt!

The jury was dismissed for lunch at noon with instructions to start deliberating at 1:30 p.m. Anna and I went for lunch. None of us, including our attorney, could read the jury as to how they might vote. This whole trial was nothing like a sporting event where one knows what the score is as the game goes along. Now "the game" was over and we had no idea who'd won.

We were shocked to get a call from my lawyer at 2:10 p.m., stating the jury had only needed thirty minutes to reach a verdict. That was a new record, according to her experience. We soon joined her and returned to the courtroom.

As the jury filed in there was no sign of the verdict in their expressions—all stone-faced. But the verdict was "NOT GUILTY OF NEGLIGENCE!" Wow! What a feeling of ecstasy as the weight fell off my shoulders. When the jury was allowed out of their seats they came down to congratulate us. Several said, "It was no contest."

With great joy and relief we gave hugs around, thanked our

attorney, and then went to the Golden Valley Clinic to share the good news. We then called our kids, went out to eat, and enjoyed a movie.

This ended my "nightmare," leaving me wiser and deeply grateful for the support of family, friends, and HSM. My prayer for the plaintiff was for her inner healing and the ability to move on in her life.

In a way, life seemed to come to a halt with the heavy burden of the malpractice suit on my shoulders. Now with joy, Anna and I looked forward to all that God had for us and our family in the future. Our thoughts turned toward our grandkids.

— 12 —

Pursuing our Grandkids

My wife and I were blessed with five children. As grandkids came along we started to wonder how to connect with them so as to be able to speak into their lives. We were especially concerned about this since all our kids had moved some distance away, for different good reasons. Since both my grandfathers had passed away ten years or so before I was born, I didn't have a clue how to stay close to these precious ones. So we prayed for wisdom and He began to show us a variety of things we could do.

The second weekend of June 2002 we visited our daughter Melanie and her family in West Des Moines, Iowa. We went with them to their place of worship, Valley Church, on that Sunday. Their pastor, Quintin Stieff, spoke from 2 Timothy 2:2 on "Persevering Vision." He posed a simple, yet profound question that was new to me. He asked, "Do you have a one hundred-year vision of anchoring your children, grandchildren and great-grandchildren in Christ?" He had read that in a book, *Anchor Man,* written by Steve Farrar. I wrote the question in my church bulletin and left it in my Bible for months. I kept ruminating on it until I had to take action.

In January 2003, we learned that three more of our grandchildren were relocating, from close to us in Minnesota, to Florida.

This meant that eleven of our twelve grandchildren at that time, were scattered across the country in various parts of California, Illinois, Florida, and Iowa.

I found myself weeping before the Lord one morning, asking that His Spirit would begin to develop this hundred-year vision in me. What does such a vision look like? Where do I start?

Ideas Flowed

A weekly letter

One week later the idea struck me to write a letter to one grandchild each week. As a doc my handwriting wasn't the best, but, if I was careful, I knew they would be able to read it or they could get help from their parents. I felt it would be more meaningful to them if they received a letter from Papa rather than an email.

After a few months a dear friend of Anna's, Lee Miller, heard what I was doing and offered a suggestion. Every time her grandfather wrote her a letter he put in a stick of gum. She thought that was real cool. I thought it was a great idea and added a stick of gum to each letter I wrote thereafter. Each grandchild became more excited when a letter from me arrived. The one exception was when Gabby had to have braces on her teeth.

"God walks"

Another piece of the vision came in February 2003. We wanted to encourage our grandkids to grow in their ability to listen and hear God's voice.

When we traveled to their respective homes I asked the parents to find a place where we could take everyone on a "God walk." This turned out to be a nature walk in a nearby park. Most of my grandkids were in the four- to ten-year-old age bracket when I started this.

At the start of the walk I shared the story in 1 Samuel 3:1–11.

The two most important words that God said to Samuel were in verse 11 (MSG), *"Listen carefully."*

We then talked about the different ways God may speak to us. Four-year-old Gabby's response was, "God speaks to us in our heart." So I encouraged everyone to listen carefully as we went on the walk. Afterward we stopped for an ice cream cone and talked about what we'd heard God say. It was a thrill to hear their responses.

After listening to the birds sing and looking at beautiful flowers, Cody, age eight, felt God said to him, "I want you to be swift and fast to help hurting people, but also soft and kind as well."

A son-in-law's observation

During the Christmas time of 2003, we had some family share time with those who were able to come. I talked about the first baby steps of my vision of connecting with our grandkids.

My son-in-law Craig responded, "Dave, those weren't baby steps but giant leaps!" He said this because of the impact he saw the letters had on his two sons.

A journal

During a series of visits during 2004, another piece of the puzzle fell into place. We had just arrived at the Los Angeles airport and were visiting my oldest son, Dan, his wife, Rose, and their two daughters, Isabel and Gabby. I rode in the backseat of the car with Isabel, age eight. She suddenly said to me, "I've been hearing from God a lot lately."

My ears perked up and I responded, "That's great Isabel. What has He been saying to you?"

Her reply was, "I forget."

A thought occurred to me, and I said, "You know, Isabel, Papa forgets many times as well unless I write it down."

In the next few days Anna and I bought journals for Isabel and

Gabby. In the front of each I wrote my desire for them to write or draw pictures of what they thought God was saying to them.

I challenged them to memorize Proverbs 3: 5–6 out of their Bible and also out of the Message Bible, *"Trust GOD from the bottom of your heart; don't try to figure out everything on your own. Listen for GOD's voice in everything you do, everywhere you go; he's the one who will keep you on track."*

As further motivation, I promised each of them that if they memorized the verses I would give them five dollars. So as we made the rounds the grandkids each got a journal and the same challenge with a promise.

A special insert in birthday cards

One day in the summer of 2004, I was looking at a picture of my grandson Elijah, who was soon to be nine years old. I began to wonder what life had been like for me when I'd turned his age, fifty-eight years previously. I knew that I had a valuable treasure in my dad's five-year diary collection dating back to 1933. The idea hit me to make a chronological listing of events that happened in my ninth year of life, as recorded by him. I did that and put it in Elijah's birthday card. I then made a similar listing for each of my years from the fourth to the thirteenth year of my life, and one from when I was sixteen. Each grandchild with a birthday in those years would get a little idea of what my life had been like in the corresponding year. It's been fun to see the interest and questions that are sparked when they get their birthday cards.

Family Reunions

As the grandkids increased in numbers and age we decided to have a family reunion every other year. We were concerned that the cousins would never get to see each other if we didn't try and bring everybody together on a somewhat regular basis. We had bought into some timeshares in the mid-1990s that allowed us to get three to four units at a given resort for a very reasonable price. We wanted the reunion to be a week in length so we would have to have it in the summertime.

We started off in 1998, having our first at Breezy Point Resort near Pequot Lakes. The next four were at Clover Ridge, Iowa, on Lake Panorama. We chose those places so we could take my boat along and enjoy various water sports.

With six different family units it was easy to take turns having one family in charge of making the evening meal for everyone. Other meals were every family for themselves, which allowed for a lot of spontaneity.

Water sports or just sitting at the beach were favorite activities. Some enjoyed golf, volley ball, going for walks, taking a nap, or whatever else was available. There were a lot of various table games played as well.

We made time for one family each evening to share their joys and struggles or whatever they were concerned about. Then we had prayer for them. We usually had a communion service once during the week. On a couple of reunions there were children who desired to be baptized by their respective dad, with my assistance. Those events were very special.

Our sixth reunion in 2008, came on the heels of celebrating our fiftieth wedding anniversary. Since everyone was in town and all wanted a different place to go, we found the Heartwood Conference Center in northwestern Wisconsin, near the town of Trego. This was a wonderful place for us. The highlight was canoeing down part of the Namekagon River. This was a river we canoed almost every year in the mid-1970s to mid-1980s with our family.

The seventh gathering was at Windham Resort in Fairfield Glade, Tennessee. The most unusual experience was visiting the Horace Burgess's Tree House at Crossville, Tennessee. It's considered the largest tree house in the world—ninety-seven feet tall, and is supported by an eighty-foot tall, white oak tree. (Google it if interested.) Horace, the builder, shared his testimony with us of how he'd felt God told him to build it. It was an amazing story.

The next one was in Colorado. We had a lovely resort with good amenities, a nearby river to float down, and different waterfalls to explore. The highlight for us was a gift that Matt and Tami devised. They had T-shirts made in the correct size for each of us with the inscription, "The 2012 McQuoid Family Reunion." The second line was, "Pagosa Springs, CO." Instead of just giving them out Tami had the idea of giving them one at a time.

We were in a large circle on a Friday evening with twenty-five people and an empty chair on one side of the ring. She or Matt would call out a name. That person would put on their T-shirt and sit in the chair. Then anyone who wanted to speak into that person's life was invited to do so. Matt and Tami led the way while others followed with what they saw in that person. It was a powerful experience as we felt the Holy Spirit flood the room.

When 2014 rolled around we had the joy of having the first wedding among our grandkids. Jacob Roberts and Lindsey Giblin were married in North Carolina. It was a beautiful wedding and brought most of our family together from all over the country. It was like a mini family reunion that went by too fast.

In June we realized that God was telling us to downsize and sell our lake home of twenty-four and a half years, so we thought we'd try a reunion at our house the last week in July. Four of our families came and helped us to get rid of things, improve the outside appearance on the lake, and take mementos that they desired. It was a fun time being together, but also a sad time as they were saying goodbye to our home.

We hope to keep having bi-annual get-togethers, but we know that as families increase with weddings and new babies it will be harder to get everyone together. However, we rejoice that we achieved our goal of getting cousins together, so they could grow up knowing and enjoying each other.

The Granddaddy Idea of all Ideas

We continued to think and pray for ways to impact our grandkids. I remember talking with a dear friend, Dick McCauley, several years ago about things he and his wife, Jean, did with theirs. As each child turned thirteen they were taken on a trip to a place of their choosing.

We thought that was a great idea and decided we would do something similar. We started with some ideas for the trip, which we wrote out and gave to the parents and grandkids when he or she was still twelve. This grew and changed as we had new thoughts and ideas.

The six points listed below have been a part of our preparation for the majority of our trips.

Our Desires

1. To have extended quality time with each one, so as to deepen our relationship with them.

2. To enjoy a part of the country he/she would like to see and activities he/she would like to do within our physical and financial capabilities. This excludes Disney World or similar amusement parks. We wanted this to be educational while exploring God's great creation somewhere in the lower forty-eight states.

3. To experience God in a deeper way by seeing His handiwork, hearing His voice, and observing His thumbprints on every aspect of the trip. A verse we will say every morning is Psalm 105:4 (MSG), *"Keep your eyes open for GOD, watch for his works; be alert for signs of his presence."* At the end of the day we would ask each other, "How did we see God today?"

4. To build Scripture into their life through Bible discussions and memorization. The passages to memorize before leaving on the trip are Psalm 119:9–11, followed by Ephesians 6:10–18.

5. To be responsible for brief morning devotions each day. This can be a verse of Scripture or something he/she has read to share with us.

6. To write in their journal about preparing for the trip (how he/she arrived at the decision of where to go), experiences on the trip, and especially how they saw or heard from God.

De-briefing

This is an important part of our trip when we return the grandchild to their parents' home. We planned on three to four days to tell all the happenings we'd had plus showing pictures. It's wonderful to hear the child tell his or her parents about the many God-sightings we had experienced. There are always stories to be told and it takes time for them to come out.

"Where Do You Go?"

When we talk about these trips with anyone they always ask, "Where do you go?" It's a delight to tell them the destination of each grandchild.

Knowing that the reader would like to see an answer to that same question, here it is:

- Jacob Roberts: 6/3/2015–6/9/2015—hiking in the northern part of the Great Smoky Mountains National Park.

- Derek Ober: 10/21/2006–10/27/2006—hiking in the southern part of the Smoky Mountains, including whitewater rafting.

- Isabel McQuoid: 6/25/2007–7/2/2007—looking for and finding the wild mustangs, especially White Cloud, in the Pryor Mountains south of Billings, Montana.

- Cody Carlson: 7/20/2007–7/28/2007—the Badlands, and the Black Hills in South Dakota, and Devil's Tower in Wyoming.

- Elijah Roberts: 7/28/2008–8/3/2008—Grand Canyon and other national parks, Petrified Forest, and Painted Desert, Arizona.

- Zach Carlson: 6/16/2009–6/23/2009—Manhattan Island, 6/23–6/28/2009—bonus time with Anna's family in New Jersey.

- Brennan Ober: 7/19/2010–7/27/2010—hiking in the Colorado Rockies, and climbing a small mountain in Colorado.

- Gabby McQuoid: 6/15/2012–6/22/2012—Cape Cod, Massachusetts, with whale watching and visiting historical sites, 6/11–6/14/2012—bonus time with Anna's family.

- Luke Roberts: 6/2/2013–6/9/2013—Charleston, South Carolina, and many Civil War sites.

- Ryley Ober: 6/14/2013–6/21/2013—Churchill Downs and several horse ranches in Kentucky.

- Rachel McQuoid: 6/28/2015–7/5/2015—Manhattan Island, 6/25–6/27/2015, and 7/6–7/8/2015—bonus time with Anna's family.

As of the writing of this book we have five more grandkids "waiting" in line for their trip over the next seven years. They are Josiah McQuoid, Grace McQuoid, Nathaniel Roberts, Benjamin McQuoid, and Chris DeAguero.

Chris is a very special grandson because he came into our family at the age of nine, with his mother, Rose, when she and our son Dan were married. He was way beyond the thirteen-year mark when we started these trips. But we love him as we love all our other grandkids. He will get his trip as well.

Both Anna and I feel the basis for our vision was Psalm 78:5–7 (MSG), *"He planted a witness in Jacob, and set his Word firmly in Israel, then commanded our parents to teach it to their children, so the next generation would know, and all the generations to come— know the truth and tell the stories, so their children can trust in God, never forget the works of God but keep his commands to the letter. Heaven forbid they should be like their parents, bullheaded and bad, a fickle and faithless bunch who never stayed true to God."*

Before I retired I remember talking with a grandfather in my office. I asked him what he was doing to stay connected with his grandkids. His response went something like this, "I am through with looking after kids. My grandkids are grown and don't need me. I have things I want to do for myself."

I felt so sad for him and his grandkids. He didn't have a clue what he was missing, much less that he was robbing his grandkids of a meaningful, and possibly life-changing relationship with their grandfather.

So to all you grandparents out there who are reading my book, there are two key words to think about—vision and intentionality. Ask God to give you the vision you need to connect with your grandkids and then be very intentional about pursuing after them.

Now, I need to shift gears a bit and write about something totally different but very crucial in family relationships. There are times when I need someone who knows me well, to hold up a mirror for me to see major flaws in my life. It's all part of God's pruning process in me.

⟼ 13 ⟻

The Gift of a Mirror

One is never too old to learn and to change if one truly wants to do so. I was presented with such an opportunity by my wife on September 6, 2008. She held up a mirror, in the form of words, so I could see something for which I was in complete denial. What she said and the way she said it, made me sit up, take notice, and seek help in making some significant behavioral changes in myself.

t was on the above date that my closest and dearest friend, my wife, Anna, gave me an incredible gift. It was a gift that hurt deeply yet opened my eyes to something I'd never seen in our whole marriage. The words she spoke revealed what she'd been experiencing the past fifty years. She had been living with a man who had anger issues, was very controlling, and who expected his agenda to be first.

Over the years, I often apologized for my anger outbursts or controlling behavior but nothing ever changed. Anna had reached a point where she didn't want to hear further apologies, but see significant change. The control issues frequently, but not solely, revolved around finances. She made the statement to me, "I do not want to keep living like this." By that she didn't mean she was considering leaving our marriage, but it was her heart's cry to me to open my eyes and see the abusiveness of my behavior. In an email to our five adult kids, she said, "I love your dad dearly, but sometimes I do not like him very much."

Eyes Opened

Receiving the gift

As I listened to her, the veil of denial dropped from my eyes and I saw what she had lived with, and it wasn't pretty. I didn't realize that when I became a "little irritated" at something she said or did, she saw it as deep-seated anger toward herself. I didn't think I was controlling but simply thought I was right about how money was spent or decisions were made. I wanted to follow my agenda even if it crossed with hers.

By the next morning, I was able to see clearly how abusive my behavior had been to her. I wept with a broken heart as I saw what she had experienced. I felt exposed, like a deep, dark closet had been opened that I didn't even know existed. I was frightened, anxious, and felt very vulnerable. As I journaled what I was feeling, I began to ask myself questions such as: "How could I have lived for fifty years with my soulmate and best friend and treated her in such a way?" "How could I be so blind?" "What is underneath my anger that I'm trying to cover up?" I began to see that below all this behavior was pride. I wanted to look good on the outside, regardless of what was going on inside.

I had seen these same behaviors in my dad, but, to my knowledge, he'd never faced up to them. I knew, however, that I needed to deal with these issues for myself as well as for my family.

I took all this "stinking thinking" and sinful behavior to the cross and confessed it. I received His forgiveness and His cleansing. That removed all the shame I was feeling but I knew that was only the first step. I had to have help to learn a new way of living, namely, trusting instead of controlling. I was willing to do whatever it took to change, knowing I would need His power at work in me to do so.

Action taken

I met with our counseling pastor at Church of the Open Door, Bob McKenna, to ask for his guidance and help. He listened attentively as I wept through my story. He gave me several options that we talked over. He then embraced me as he prayed for divine guidance on this journey ahead. Bob had a term for my behavior—objective impairment. I think he was trying to be nice because I saw it as "thickheaded denial."

I felt led to begin the twelve-step program at our church, now known as Firstlight, which is similar to an Alcoholic Anonymous program but with a distinctive Christian perspective. I originally thought it was only for those who struggled with alcohol, drug, or sexual addiction. I quickly learned that it was, and is, for any person with an addiction or compulsive behavior who truly wants to change.

The Road to Recovery

The first step was initially hard for me to accept. I needed to admit that I was powerless over my addiction to food as my drug of choice, my behavior of anger, control, agenda issues, and my judgmental attitude toward others; simply that my life had become unmanageable. I didn't like to admit I was powerless. My pride was still raising its ugly head. Eventually I came to the point of fully embracing that step.

I worked each step in the context of weekly teachings, followed by gender specific small groups. In my group I met, listened to, and shared with brothers in Christ. Their issues were different than mine, but all desired change and inner healing. These men were a great encouragement to me. Our journey together made it clear that I was not alone. Change did come, but slowly. As we learned, it takes one to two years to build new neural pathways in our brains, resulting in new ways of thinking and living. This is all empowered by the Holy Spirit.

One day as I was journaling about my issues, I realized how control and trust are the exact opposite. They are diametrically opposed to each other; like oil and water, they just don't mix. As I gave up control and embraced trusting God, I started to notice an inner freedom, lightness, and joy developing in my spirit. I also realized something else.

Interruptions

I noticed that interruptions were frequently trigger points for anger and control issues to surface. I didn't like it when something unexpected blew up my agenda for the day. I wanted to be in control, and when I wasn't I became frustrated.

Here was where the serenity prayer, which we quoted at our weekly meetings, had an impact on me. I added four words to the first part of the prayer so I said it like this: "God grant me the serenity to accept the things I cannot change (interruptions), the courage to change the things I can (my attitude toward interruptions), and the wisdom to know the difference. . . ." I would quote this, plus the rest of the prayer, every time I went on my morning walk.

During my morning time with the Lord, I learned to turn my day over to Him, welcoming any interruptions that might come my way. Practicing this discipline helped me become more aware of His presence throughout the day.

As I wrote about this in my journal recently, a "light bulb" flipped on in my mind, giving me a deeper insight. It was possible to take an interruption and turn it into a divine appointment if I did two things. First, I needed to remember that this was His day and *"that God causes all things to work together for good"* (Romans 8:28a NASB), even if a negative circumstance appeared on my plate.

Second, I could choose to either be frustrated about the situation or *"Rejoice in the Lord always; again I will say, rejoice!"* (Philippians 4:4, NASB). I needed to realize that He probably did not bring the interruption but He was in it. As I let that sink in, I could only rejoice. The result was, I had joy and peace.

This leads me to a final story in this chapter.

The dishwasher story

I had been faithfully working the program a year and a half or so and was wondering if I was making progress. One day in the late morning, I was in the kitchen loading the dishwasher. When I tried to start it nothing happened. I pushed all the buttons but to no avail. I called Anna to see if she had the "magic touch" to get it going. She had no luck. I had a list of things to do that day and didn't have time for the dishwasher not to work. I started to feel frustrated, but then I paused, took a deep breath and remembered I had given the day to God, so He was in charge of my day, not me. I chose to rejoice that He had things under control. I was filled with peace and joy. What a totally new experience for me.

I got out the dishwasher manual and found the 800 number for the service department. The service tech was very helpful as he walked me through what needed to be done. It took a couple of phone calls to him, but three hours later the dishwasher was working like new. I rejoiced that not only did the dishwasher work, but I had remained calm, peaceful, and full of joy. Anna rejoiced with me as well. Healing from past behavior was definitely occurring.

So have I arrived? Far from it! I know there are more layers of the "ole onion" that in time need to be peeled off. I also know that as I continue pursuing God, His Spirit will gently and lovingly reveal them to me. Then I have the choice to remain the same or to pursue wholeness. I strongly desire the latter. This is all a part of the purifying process.

I have peace and take great hope from 1 Peter 5:10 (NASB, my emphasis), *"And after you have struggled for a little while, the God of all grace who called you to His eternal glory in Christ, will Himself, perfect, confirm, strengthen and establish you."*

This journey of recovery has truly opened my eyes to the wonderful challenge of learning to put my trust in Him. God is so trustworthy and so good. Why would I ever think I could do "whatever" better than He could? He, who loves me unconditionally and lovingly, prunes me, and is wonderful and good beyond words. The result is that I'm hungry and thirsty for more of Him.

— 14 —

Thirsting for More

I've had a desire for more of God even when I was following the wrong god. It intensified after I met the God of Grace. I was, and still am, so grateful we were at Church of the Open Door because of the worship, the grace-filled messages, and so many opportunities to connect with fellow seekers after God in fellowship and service. That all increased my thirst for Him. But God had more for me to learn. My son Matt and his wife, Tami, invited us to Miracles in the Market Place International four years ago. There I have seen and experienced more of the Holy Spirit that has made me cry out for still more.

As I look back over my life, I feel there was a yearning to know God in increasingly deeper ways. That desire got all messed up with my trying to look good on the outside and my performance mindset. This was because most of my life I'd had the wrong view of God. After I met the God of Grace, I experienced a gradual freedom from shame, performance, and trying to look good. What a joy it was to realize and embrace the truth that God loved me unconditionally, wanted intimacy with me, and was profoundly proud of me, in spite of the "warts" I still had.

I grew in my thirst for God's Word, His love letters to me. I enjoyed finding Scripture that spoke to my heart, memorizing the passage and then passing it on to others, especially my grandkids. Zephaniah 3:17 (NASB) was such a verse, *"The Lord your God is with you, He is mighty to save. He will take great delight in you, He will quiet you with His love, He will rejoice over you with singing."*

That verse impacted me deeply then and still does. My daughter Debbie did a needlepoint of that verse and gave it to me as a birthday gift, months after I'd had met the God of Grace. Many times I've just wept as I've let the meaning of that verse sink deeper into my spirit and soul.

It was some years later when out for a morning walk, I was drawn to a beautiful bird in a tree next to the path I was on. As I recall, it was a cardinal singing at the top of his lungs. I stopped and just looked at him as he kept on singing. Then this revelation hit me: That bird is God's special messenger He sent to sing over me as Zephaniah recorded. I was moved to tears.

When we visited our grandkids, it was a great joy to tell them about what I'd experienced. Then I took them on a nature walk to hear God's songbirds sing over them. I told them what Zephaniah said, *"He takes great delight in you and rejoices over you with singing,"* because you are His very special creation.

As important as God's precious promises are to me, and there are many that I treasure in my heart, I also needed supportive people for encouragement to face the challenges that lay ahead. That came in many various ways but all stirred up in me a thirst and hunger for more of Him.

Church of the Open Door

Men's Group

About twenty years ago I felt a hunger to connect with some Christian men on a weekly basis. I didn't want Bible study, as such, but I wanted to connect with men who were willing to do life together. I found three or four guys who were interested.

Our format was simple. Since men rarely talk about emotions, we decided to go around the circle and each share three feelings we were in touch with. The second go-around each man shared what was behind those feelings. We found, since all agreed to confidentiality and the willingness not to try and fix anyone, we went quite deep with each other. What a precious time. We always ended in prayer for each other.

Over the years men have come and gone, but there have always been two to four who desire to meet on a Saturday morning. The fellowship has been rich and life-giving.

Restoration Through Prayer (RTP)

As I was slowing down in my medical practice in 1999, Anna and I felt a yearning to be involved in a ministry together. That led us to the Restoration Through Prayer ministry led by Peggy Lang and Lynn Casale. This became a rich learning experience for us through the monthly training sessions taught by our very capable leaders and the hands-on praying for others. Our usual appointment times were Monday evenings for an hour and a half. Initially we had two appointments per night but in the last few years we've reduced it.

The powerful thing for us has been to realize it's not about us, but all about Him. He always precedes us in the lives of those individuals coming for prayer. Our challenge is to prayerfully discern how we fit into what God has already been doing. Our initial prayer is always, "Holy Spirit, come." Many times our next prayer is, "Help," because we don't know what direction we should go. But we know that He will show up and give us the words to say or pray. Many times it's all about listening and very little talking. In most cases, at the end of the session the individual has felt His touch and leaves with a sense of peace and joy. We likewise are grateful for the privilege of knowing God partnered with us in this prayer session.

We have further enjoyed praying for people at the altar after morning service. That has also been a rich experience of seeing God at work.

Top Secret

In the summer of 2004, Open Door pastors Al Schuck and Tom McCullough invited Rick Patton and myself to co-lead a class of dads. The overall purpose was to develop a curriculum that would encourage fathers to become very intentional in calling out their sons into godly manhood. The goal was to let the class size develop and grow gradually as God led, without significant church awareness, hence the name "Top Secret."

As we felt the challenge in calling us to do this we soon discovered that Top Secret became a living organism as it grew and changed with each class. The growth in depth was due to the constructive evaluations of the dads, along with Spirit-led ideas that came to us. Each class started in September and ended in May, with two meetings a month. We had four to seven dads in each class, geared for fathers with twelve- to thirteen-year-old sons.

It was a thrill to see how the dads became very intentional in reaching out to their sons. The principles they applied to their sons also extended to their daughters. The testimonials of the value of the program five and ten years later were very precious and powerful. I was so grateful to be a part of nine classes when I sensed the Holy Spirit's redirection in my life to start writing this book. Top Secret went one more year and then closed when Rick was led to another ministry.

In the ten years that Top Secret existed, over fifty dads were touched and challenged to pursue their sons. The ripple effect will only be known in eternity.

Community Group

It was nine-plus years ago that my wife and I began longing to connect with a group of people within Open Door. Our thirst was for community where friendships could go to a deeper level. We knew that our good friends Dave and Jan Nelson had been leading a community group for several years, which met once a month and was open to new people. We decided to check them out.

It was a "go" from the very first visit, especially since we already knew some of the people. We have thoroughly enjoyed the friendship, fellowship, and openness of the group. Heavy things are shared comfortably, knowing that prayer will be offered on behalf of the one sharing. It's been a rich experience to go deeper with a group of sojourners in this walk through life.

Miracles in the Marketplace International

What stirred in me

In April 2011, Rachel McQuoid went to her mom asking to be baptized. She was nine years old. Matt and Tami, her parents, had been attending a Thursday evening healing service for some time, known as "Miracles in the Marketplace," led by Craig and Suzy Nelson. Tami asked Craig if he would baptize Rachel, to which he gave an enthusiastic, "Yes." They invited us to attend.

It was a wonderful service, the likes of which I'd never been in before. There was a short worship time and message. Then Pastor Craig asked Matt and Tami to stand up, where he proceeded to speak powerful, prophetic words over them.

He then did the same to Anna and myself. I was blown away. He saw a mentoring gift in me to the younger generations. I could see that was because of the Top Secret ministry I was in with other dads. He also saw a wisdom gift that he thought was extraordinary and he encouraged me to start writing.

I didn't resonate with that at the time. Now that I've felt called to write this book and am almost done I feel he was spot-on.

After the baptism there was a communion service where each one who took part was prayed over. What a powerful experience as well. Early in the service Craig made the statement that "Many of us live in a measure of the Holy Spirit, while it's God's desire for us to live in the fullness of His Spirit." That service stirred in me a longing for more of the Holy Spirit.

I began to attend MIMI as often as possible. I saw many physical healings, which amazed me. From time to time, I would bring a friend with a physical ailment to the Thursday service for prayer. Not all were healed, but everyone was touched by the prayer offered on their behalf. I've been impacted personally by prayer from groups of people that have gathered around me asking for healing in some of my health issues.

Divine appointments

I will say more of this in my epilogue, but I wanted to say here what a joy it's been to reach out to people when nudged by the Holy Spirit. I've learned that if I ask God for a divine appointment at the start of the day, it's amazing to see how He answers and leads me to someone who needs a special touch of God's love, be it prayer, words of encouragement, or whatever. I'll share a couple of unusual encounters.

It was a beautiful day in May 2011 when I started my morning walk after asking for a divine appointment. As I neared the end of my walk I noticed a neighbor friend with her blue merle collie dog, Gypsy, up ahead. As I approached Leah I noticed Gypsy was lying on the grass. When out for a walk I'd never seen her lying down. As I drew closer I asked Leah if Gypsy, who was ten years old, was getting older and needed to rest.

With a very concerned look on her face, she said, "No, she has cancer, adenocarcinoma of the intestine. She could have surgery tomorrow, next week, or I could just keep her comfortable. She's lost fifteen pounds, is getting weaker almost every day, and hardly eats anything."

As she talked I knew this was the divine appointment I had

requested. So I asked Leah if I could pray for her Gypsy. She responded positively so I knelt next to this beautiful creation of God, gently petted her, and prayed. I asked for Jesus to come touch her, destroy all cancer cells, and give her new life.

When I was through an interesting thing happened. Gypsy got up on her front legs and touched my chin with her nose. Leah said, "Look, she's saying thank you." Then with hope in her eyes, Leah went on to say, "I've just decided that I'm going to take her to have surgery tomorrow." She was very grateful and thanked me deeply from her heart.

A couple of weeks later a very nice thank you note from Leah appeared in our mailbox. She wrote, "I wanted you to know that Gypsy is doing really well after her surgery. She ended up with a sarcoma, which was completely removed. There was no lymph node involvement. Her lungs, liver, spleen, et cetera, were all clear! Can you believe it? This was not the outcome I expected. I really believe, Dave, your prayer was heard. I am so grateful, and I really believe God intervened with your help."

Gypsy lived another full year before passing. More than once Leah has said to me that it was the prayer that made the difference.

I agree with her, although it was not about me, but the God who loves all His creation passionately.

The second divine appointment made me laugh and realize God has a wonderful sense of humor. Anna and I were having breakfast at McDonald's when I sensed the Spirit nudge me to talk to a gentleman in a booth near by. I prayed as I approached him, and with a smile, I said, "My wife and I enjoy praying for people. Is there anything that we could pray about for you?"

He looked at me with a smile on his face and answered, "No speak-a-da English."

I'm sure I had a surprised look, but with a smile, I said, "I want you to know how much God loves you."

He smiled back, "No speak-a-da English."

I smiled, shook his hand, and returned to my booth laughing. Anna had a good chuckle also. For a brief moment I thought, "Why did the Spirit send me to him?"

Yet the answer is obvious. God's love is communicated whether you speak the other person's language or not. That gentleman needed a touch of God's love and he received it. This hankering to reach out to people with God's love came through challenges from the leaders in what is now called Miracles in the Marketplace International.

As I close this chapter, I fully sense that my hungering and thirsting for more of Him continues unabated. I'm drawn to a verse in Ephesians 2:10 (NASB), *"For we are His workmanship, created in Christ Jesus for good works, which God prepared beforehand, that we should walk in them."* I am awestruck as I try to let in the truth that God has prepared "good works" for me to do from before creation. Now I have the joy to walk in them and, with His power, accomplish them. I feel strongly that He has many more tasks for me to do before He calls me home. I look forward to seeing what they are and then partnering with Him in accomplishing them. I know that the best is yet to come!

⇥ 15 ⇤

The Best is Yet to Come

When I retired from medicine in May 2005, I knew that God had more for me to do. My desire was and is to be like Caleb, one of my favorite Bible characters, who "wholly followed the Lord my God" Joshua 14:6–14 (KJV). The first of sixteen grandparenting trips started after I retired. Now this book, which has been a passion of mine to write for quite some time, is becoming a reality. This has been a good start but I know He has more for me to do.

felt very blessed to work in a profession that I really enjoyed. I loved being a family physician and caring for the whole family, including obstetrics. Many times I was asked, "If I had life to do over, would I do something different?"

My answer was always, "No way, I enjoyed being a family doc." Sure, there were challenges and difficulties along the road but that's the reality with any job or profession.

However, there comes a time when one begins to slow down and think about retirement. Our family practice at the Golden Valley Clinic of four family docs, was sold to Park Nicollet Clinic in St. Louis Park, Minnesota, in the spring of 1992. I agreed to sign a seven-year contract as an employee of the clinic.

As I approached the end of my contract, I didn't feel ready to leave medicine completely. So I chose to retire from my family practice the end of April 1999. I was sixty-two and a half years of age and still able to do Urgent Care medicine for Park Nicollet. That eliminated hospital work, a daily list of patient phone calls, and since I was president of the clinic, a lot of administrative work. I was glad to give all that up.

I found that I really enjoyed doing Urgent Care, so much so, that I often said, "I wish I'd started doing this sooner." I worked half-time for a few years and then cut back to quarter-time and finally settled on four-hour shifts three times a week. I felt like I could keep doing that for years, but God had other plans.

In early April 2005 I began to sense a nudging in my spirit that I should consider quitting completely. One day I asked Anna what she would like me to do. With tears in her eyes she said, "I want you to quit."

My response was, "Okay, I will!" I thought, because of the Urgent Care schedule, I would need to work through June. So that's what I told Anna.

I decided to take a couple of days at a retreat center to reflect on the forty-three years of medicine that I had practiced. I felt some sadness saying goodbye, but I knew God was in this decision. I knew He would take the passion He had created me with, and redirect it into something different, new, and wonderful. When I asked God, "What's next?" I sensed in my spirit that He said, "Just rest and spend time with Me."

I was surprised when I also sensed on that retreat, He wanted May 31, 2005, to be my last day of work. A quick phone call to the Urgent Care scheduler revealed that was possible. Then I felt impressed with the idea of inviting our five kids to surprise their mom by coming for a Mother's Day celebration on Friday, May 6. Three of the five could make it. So we had a surprise party for her at Matt and Tami's home in Chanhassen, Minnesota. Anna was thrilled when we arrived at their home, thinking we were going to babysit their kids. Instead, she was shocked to see that Dan was there from California, Melanie from Iowa, along with Matt and Tami, to help her celebrate my retirement. She was further surprised and thrilled when she opened my envelope to find my Urgent Care schedule ending on May 31 instead of the last of June.

The amazing thing to us was, after my last day of work, the very next day, June 1, we left on our first grandparenting trip.

As my focus shifted from "my" doing medicine to "our" going on grandparenting trips, I had the strong sense the practice of medicine was a closed chapter. Now Anna and I had entered this new season of our life together, part of which was connecting with our grandkids in a deeper way. We looked forward to this next phase with joy and anticipation.

It was then that I began to wonder about the challenge of leaving a legacy for the next generation and the ones that follow.

Writing this Book

The first steps

As I neared my retirement in 2005, I started writing stories about my childhood years and the crazy things my brother, Bill, and I did. I was writing just for fun and sent them to family members. I got the feedback, "You can really write." Initially I discounted that observation.

Then I wrote a couple of articles, "Noticing Things from Nature," and "A Grandfather's Journey." These were published in our church paper *Kingdom Now*.

I sent the grandfather article to a dear friend of mine, Don Anderson. He and his wife, Cara, were members at a Covenant church in Denver, Colorado. Don suggested I send my article to the monthly publication of his denomination, *The Covenant Companion*. I did and it was published in their June 2005 issue.

The idea that I could write a book still had never entered my mind.

A challenging goal

I continued to write short stories because I enjoyed writing. My family, especially my daughter-in-law Tami, kept "bugging" me saying, "You've got a book in you, start writing."

I noticed in a Robbinsdale school listing of events the opportunity to attend a memory writer class for three to four weeks. I signed up for it. That stimulated me to do more writing. Four of us in that class decided to meet monthly to share our writings and critique them for each other. We stayed together for a year and a half before it dissolved for various reasons.

It was somewhere during the year of 2011 when I began to wonder if I could write a book. The more I thought about it and talked it over with Anna, the more I felt drawn to give it a try. I knew that a passion was growing in me to share about my life with my grandkids. I wanted to get started but wasn't sure how to do it.

There's a well-known proverb, the origin of which is debated, which states, "When the student is ready, the teacher will appear." That was certainly true in my case.

Some time in the early spring of 2012, I met David Sluka at MIMI. He was helping out the worship team by playing the keyboard. Initially I didn't know that he was a writer, speaker, author, and coach, who has helped many people in their writings. Since he's a teacher at heart he enjoys having writers workshops. I learned he was having one April 12. I signed up.

What a wonderful experience that turned out to be for me. I came away with ten things I wanted to talk about in my book, ten chapter titles, and a brief summary of each chapter. I was so grateful for that day.

It took a while to get into the rhythm of writing. My biggest struggle was being distracted. Important things would come along that I had to handle. I also had some not so important matters that I let rob my time, such as watching a sporting event on TV.

It was almost a year later, as I approached the end of the ninth class of dads I was co-leading, that I felt the Spirit nudge me with a question: "Is it time to bow out of the Top Secret ministry and devote more time to writing?" Though it was hard, I knew it was the right thing to do. I resigned.

The key event that really impelled my writing occurred on Wednesday, January 15, 2014. The Twin Cities Prophetic Conference was starting at the Redeemer Love Church in St. Paul, sponsored by MIMI. I had volunteered to help with the ushering so I arrived about 4:30 p.m. As I walked through the gathering place toward the auditorium I noticed some people in an overflow or classroom area. I saw David Sluka up front of the group and realized that he was finishing up a writers workshop.

After the class dispersed I was able to chat with him. He said, "I have your book."

He had contacted me and several others who had been at his 2012 workshop. He'd asked permission to use a small part of the workshop that each of us had written, in his book he was writing. His offer was that everyone who had his work chosen would receive a free book of his. He had emailed me sometime in the summer of 2013 that I was a winner. I looked forward to receiving his book.

I had been floundering a bit in my writing at that point. I needed some step-by-step direction. His book gave that to me. I felt it was clearly a God-thing that I would run into him at that conference.

For me, one of the most inspiring writings in David's book, *Write Your Book**, was chapter five titled "Write Inspired and Write with God." He stated, "God wants to help you write," and "God wants

---

* David J. Sluka, *Write Your Book: Your Step-by-Step Guide to Write and Publish a Great Nonfiction Book* (Bloomington, MN: Hit The Mark Publishing, 2014), 35–36.

to write through you and with you." I have experienced that totally. Every time I sit down to write I sense His presence. I love to sit there praying, "Holy Spirit, dictate to me." I've learned that if I'm in a difficult place in my writing I need to pause and ask for His direction. As I wait I receive ideas that clarify what I should say next.

Another thing that has helped me was a CD of a Christian writer saying to, "Treat your writing like a job. Plan when you will go to work and when you will come home." What that looks like for me is to get up about 4:30 a.m., have some quiet time, give the day to God for Him to direct my steps, and then start writing. Initially my goal was to write five hours per day, five days a week. Frequently during the first six months of 2014, I reached that goal. Other times, two to three hours per day was all I got in but my goal remained the same.

After I received David Sluka's book I set a goal of having the manuscript down by mid-September, followed by the complete book by Christmas, Lord willing. I was chugging right along like the train engine in the child's book, *The Little Engine That Could*, saying as he chugged up the mountain, "I think I can, I think I can." Then in mid-June, Anna and I realized we were facing a very significant mountain in our lives. Here is where a powerful proverb that we often quote came into play. Proverbs 16:9 (NASB), "*The mind of man plans his way but the LORD directs his steps.*"

One day Anna came to the startling discovery that our finances were going in the red, which I'll get into more in the epilogue. But as we were faced with the need to downsize and sell our home it became very clear to us that God was redirecting our plans with His steps. I had to take a six-month break from writing. The goal of having the book by Christmas of that year went out the window. The new goal was the fall or winter of 2015.

A writers group

I had seen in Open Doors' periodic supplement of events a writers group that met twice a month. The first couple of times

I saw the notice I dismissed it as not something for me. When I looked at it in May of 2014 I had a different reaction. This time I thought, "I should check this out to see if it would be helpful." I contacted the person listed and was welcomed to visit the next meeting.

I found this to be a wonderful group because we critiqued each other's writing offering suggestions for improvement. That has been an education for me.

However, it's more than just a writers group, it's a community of people who care for each other. We share our ups and downs. At the end of the meeting, prayer requests are given and we pray for each other. It has been a rich experience.

An Unexpected Development in My Journey

Dan's recommendation

As Anna and I were preparing for a trip to California in the fall of 2009 to visit our son Dan and his family, he made a suggestion. Since my dad developed dementia during the last five years of his life, passing at age ninety-one, Dan had thought that it would be a good idea for both of us to have a baseline study of our cognitive ability. Dan has his PsyD degree and practices psychology in Southern California. He has used Dr. William Shankle, a neurologist who specialized in dementia, in evaluating some of his clients.

We agreed to see him. Anna was normal and I had a mild cognitive impairment known as MCI. He recommended brain exercises. A one-year follow-up showed no change.

A sobering diagnosis

It was at my December 2013 visit that Dr. Shankle saw some change. He wanted a specialized MRI of my brain and further blood tests. It took a while for all the tests to come back.

On February 7, 2014, Anna and I had a conference call with

Dr. Shankle and my son Dan. Dr. Shankle informed us that I had early Alzheimer's Disease (AD). He placed me on appropriate medication to delay the progression of the disease. He also advised physical exercises and brain exercises known as Lumosity. Writing this book has also been an excellent brain exercise.

Embracing the diagnosis

Needless to say, it was a shock receiving that diagnosis. It did send me into a tailspin for a few days.

Then I took my eyes off myself, refocused them on God and His promises. My sadness and depression left. I knew God didn't cause the AD but He was with me in it. Ephesians 2:10 (NASB) came to mind assuring me that He had much ahead for me to do: *"For we are His workmanship, created in Christ Jesus for good works, which God prepared beforehand so that we would walk in them."*

I was blessed and encouraged by all my family's support. Melanie felt the diagnosis, "Was a blessing allowed by God to give you focus for what you need to do now: One, continue writing your book and, two, follow the instructions outlined by Dr. Shankle to slow the progress."

A month later the Spirit took me into deeper insight of how God wanted to use my AD for His glory and my good. I was up early spending time in His presence when I sensed the Spirit say to me, *"You have accepted the diagnosis but you have not embraced it."* I mused over that for a while until He brought a Scripture to my mind: 2 Corinthians 4:16–18 (NASB), *"Therefore we do not lose heart, but though our outer man is decaying, yet our inner man is being renewed day by day. For momentary, light affliction is producing for us an eternal weight of glory, far beyond all comparison, while we look not at the things that are seen, but at the things which are not seen; for the things which are seen are temporal, but the things that are not seen are eternal."*

What struck me the most was verse 17. I don't know what the apostle Paul, who wrote this book, meant by "momentary, light affliction," whether it was all of life or something else, but what it meant to me was my AD. Then Paul goes on and says (my paraphrase), *"Is producing in me an eternal weight of glory."* Now I don't know exactly what that is but it has to be awfully good. Because Paul says it is, *"Far beyond all comparison."*

I like the MSG paraphrase of this verse, *"These hard times are small potatoes compared to the coming good times, the lavish celebration prepared for us."*

When I let that into my spirit, soul, and body I melted into tears. I was blown away with His goodness and incredible love for me. I weep, even now as I write this.

To take something as undesirable as Alzheimer's and see it turned into an instrument that brings hope, joy, and peace is something that only God can do. That is what Romans 8:28 (NASB) is all about, *"And we know that God causes all things to work together for good to those who love God, to those who are called according to His purpose."*

I want to be very clear that I'm not embracing AD in and of itself, but I am embracing the way God is using this in my life to go deeper into intimacy with Him and to trust in Him more. Something else came to me as I write this section of the book.

I pray that many of you who read this book will be challenged to turn your life over to Christ if you have never done so. That would be a life-changing experience for you. I also pray that those of you who have a faith in Christ will be challenged to go deeper in your walk with Him.

A silent retreat

Over the years I've enjoyed going to Pacem In Terris north of Anoka, Minnesota, for a personal retreat. It is a Franciscan center of spirituality that welcomes guests who seek to be alone with

God. I had a longing to go for a retreat in mid-May for that purpose. I wanted to spend time with Him and talk with Him about my AD.

It was a beautiful three days in this wooded area with lots of sunshine, cool breeze, and temperature in the mid-70s. I had my own hermitage cabin for one person. There were nice trails to walk, so Friday morning I was walking one of the trails when I came to a small, shallow lake, with a lot of marsh between land and the open water. There was a boardwalk out to the open water with a steel chair and small table bolted down at the end. I sat down in the chair and just took some deep breaths. It was so serene and beautiful I felt like I could sit there all day. It was a beautiful place to sit, meditate, read, and enjoy God's presence.

I began praying about my AD. I thanked Him for the improvement both Anna and I had seen since being on the medication prescribed, along with doing the brain exercises. We both believed this was the start of His healing process in me. I also thanked Him for the inner working He had been doing in me since the diagnosis.

Then I was struck with this thought, which I believe was His Spirit speaking, "*Since you will see Dr. Shankle in the fall, why don't you begin to ask Me to surprise him? Ask Me to not only stop the progression of the AD in your brain, but to back it up two steps: One, minimal cognitive impairment where you were in 2009, and two, normal brain function.*" I was blown away and began weeping as I received what He said to me.

As I sat there in His presence, the account of King Hezekiah in the Old Testament (2 Kings 20:1–11; Isaiah 38:1–8) came to my mind. The king was mortally ill and Isaiah told him to get his house in order as he would soon die. King Hezekiah called out to God in tears. God heard his cry and told Isaiah to tell the king he would be healed and live fifteen more years. Then King Hezekiah asked for a sign to assure himself that this would happen. So Isaiah told the king that as a sign the shadow from the sun on the sundial would go forward ten degrees or backward ten degrees, whichever he chose. King Hezekiah said, in effect, that it would be easier for the sun's shadow to go forward, so he wanted to see it go backward. Isaiah then cried out to the Lord and He moved the shadow on the sundial back ten degrees.

I believe the Spirit brought that account of King Hezekiah to my mind as a confirmation that I had heard correctly. God wanted to back my AD up two stages, so I began to pray that my Abba would answer my request for complete healing. I know this was one of those things that is *"immeasurably more than all we can ask or imagine"* (Ephesians 3:20 NIV). I then got up from my chair and walked back to my hermitage, rejoicing and praising God.

I shared this encounter first with Anna by phone, then with Joe, a new friend on the staff at Pacum In Terris, and with another friend once I returned home. The first comment each of them gave was, "Wow!"

My next appointment with Dr. Shankle was January 7, 2015. We spent most of December visiting our two sons, Matt and his family in northern California, and Dan and his family in southern California. We had a wonderful time with both families. As I thought of the upcoming appointment I remained at peace, knowing that God was in control. I was curious, however, as to what Dr. Shankle would find.

On Monday evening, January 5, I developed a horrible cold and was up most of the night coughing. To let Anna sleep, I went into the family room of Dan and Rosa's home and kept praying for healing. It was a rough night and Tuesday wasn't any better. I became concerned that I might not be able to see Dr. Shankle. Sometime during the day I asked Anna to pray over me, which she did. By late evening I could tell the healing had started. I began feeling better and my cough decreased and my nose stopping running. I slept like a baby that night. The next morning I felt 85 percent recovered. That was the shortest cold I've ever had in my life.

Dr. Shankle's appointment

The appointment turned out rather amazing. The cognitive testing looked at seven different areas of my brain function. Compared to the findings the year before, four were improved, two were the same, and one was somewhat worse. Dr. Shankle attributed the one that wasn't as good to my recent head cold. His summary statement was, "You showed dramatic improvement and executive function and verbal fluency and in multitasking."

I asked him if he was surprised at my improvement. He wouldn't admit to that but felt the Lumosity exercises and the medication made the difference. I missed the opportunity to tell him that the most important factor was all the people I had behind me praying. I won't miss that opportunity ever again.

He went on to say that my improvement made him question if I truly had AD. He wanted me to enroll in a nationwide imaging study that would definitely confirm or exclude the diagnosis, giving me the information for the study.

Confirmation

After we returned to cold and snowy Minnesota, I tried to sign up for his study but it was already full. Initially I was disappointed until I found the same study in Orlando, Florida. I called and was accepted. It turned out to be a real plus because we got to spend time with some of our family living in Florida, along with other family members that came down from South Carolina for a week.

The imaging study covered a three-week period of time, with all sorts of tests. The key one was the Florbetapir PET (positron emission tomography) scan. I had no side effects from any of the "stuff" they put into me, for which I was grateful.

I was told I would have the results in two or three weeks. I guess research wheels go slow because I got my results two months later. The report confirmed the diagnosis of Alzheimer's Disease.

Was I discouraged or sad? Not at all. I was grateful for a clear-cut, black and white statement of what was in my brain.

I had so many people praying for me individually or in groups that I felt blessed to no end, and still do. I was confident that in His time and way He would restore my brain back to the two stages He'd asked me to request. I don't ask anymore, I simply thank Him that the healing is coming.

A friend in a group who prayed for me this past summer made the comment, "It's good you had the PET scan so it's well documented. When healing comes the doctors will be really shocked." I hadn't thought of it that way but I fully agreed.

I do know that God has many "good works" for me to do before He calls me home, as He has for all of His children. This book is one of them. But I want to share with you a God-thing that came totally out of the blue. I'd have never guessed it was coming, but it was one of the "good works."

The Traveling Doctor's Bag

I entered our church the first Sunday in June 2014, by myself as my dear wife was out of town. A good friend, Steve Hansen, executive director of "Beyond Our Door Global," a mission outreach primarily to Haiti, Uganda, and Kenya, intercepted me. He wanted to know where he could get some instruments for a doctor's bag, such as an otoscope. One of the Haitian young men he knew, Bruno Exame, was entering the internship part of medical school in Port-au-Prince, Haiti. Steve wanted to surprise and bless Bruno with such a gift.

So I suggested he check out a medical supply place to find such things. I guessed that a new otoscope might now cost close to two hundred dollars, but I really didn't know. Steve gulped a little bit in response as I went on into the service, which was just starting.

At home, later in the day, I began dreaming about my visit with

Steve and was hit with a thought that I believe came from the Holy Spirit. *"Why don't you give Steve your doctor's bag to give to this Haitian young man? You don't need it anymore."* I was rather stunned by the idea.

I went upstairs to the closet where I kept my bag, opened it, and laid the contents on the bed. The main instrument was a handle that held two D batteries to which either an otoscope or an ophthalmoscope head could be attached. Both still worked very well. I had several different-sized green, plastic, funnel-like attachments for the head of the otoscope, which allowed me to look at a patient's eardrums. I also had a couple of stethoscopes, blood pressure cuffs, reflex hammers, tongue blades, bandage scissors, tape measure, a small jar of alcohol, and other useful items. As I looked at the instruments in the bag I knew I wanted to give them to Bruno. I began weeping with joy as I thought of passing my bag to this aspiring young man.

Then I went downstairs and called Steve and asked him if he would like to have my doctor's bag to give to the medical student, because I really no longer had any use for it, especially since all of my grandkids and their parents had moved away. I told Steve that the otoscope and ophthalmoscope heads, along with the handle and batteries, were archaic by US standards. I had purchased them in the fall of 1957, when I started medical school at the University of Minnesota. However, they certainly were still useable and were probably of value in a third world country.

To say the least, Steve was delighted. He had planned a trip to Haiti on Friday and said he'd stop by and pick up the bag in the next day or two so he could take it with him.

When Steve arrived the next morning, I laid out all the contents of my bag on our dining room table, explaining what each one was and how to use it. As he looked at the various items I said, "There's a very interesting and rather amazing story about my first doctor's bag and the otoscope/ophthalmoscope instrument I'd like to tell you."

The first bag, with similar contents listed above, went with me through medical school, one year of internship, and then seven years in Littlefork, Minnesota, where I had my first medical practice beginning in July 1962. It went with me and my family to Congo, Africa, seven years later for a year of medical missionary work at Ruanguba. It also traveled to Uganda and Kenya. I still had the bag when I returned to the US and joined the Golden Valley Clinic in the fall of 1970.

But in November 1973 the bag and its contents left me. At the time, the Golden Valley Clinic doctors I practiced with had an office in Golden Valley and one in Camden, a subdivision of Minneapolis near the Mississippi River. On that particular day I was working at our Camden office. I'd left my medical bag on the backseat of my car, but when I came out at the end of the day I found the right rear window of my car broken and the bag missing. I called the police and an officer stopped by.

As he surveyed the situation he said, "Well, it looks to me like a 'druggie' probably thought you had drugs in your bag that he could use for himself." In case at some future time the bag would turn up, he filed a report.

Approximately six months later, a police officer walked into the Camden Clinic asking for Dr. McQuoid. Fortunately, I was working in that office on that day. As I walked toward him I saw that he had something in his hand, wrapped with a towel. When I reached him he opened up the towel.

"Holy moly, that's my bag," I said. "Where in heck did you find that?"

He laughed and said, "Well, a fisherman was trying his luck from the Camden bridge over the Mississippi. He hooked something, which he initially thought was a big fish, except it didn't fight very much. He was shocked to find that it was a doctor's bag. So he turned it into our office."

My name was on the outside of the bag and there was a soggy

ID inside. Thanks to the police report the previous November, the officer knew where to go to return it.

Needless to say, the contents were a mess and rather stinky as well. The bag and everything, except for the otoscope/ophthalmoscope, was ruined. I was able to clean them up, dry them out, and put in new bulbs and batteries and they both worked like new. The previous Christmas Anna had given me a very nice gift—another doctor's bag. I'd purchased the other items needed and was back in business with my second bag.

This new bag has been with me since then. It went with me on a medical missions trip to Honduras with Becky in 1982, to the Dominican Republic with Melanie in 1986, to Tricotte, Haiti, with Anna and Matt in 1990, and with Anna to Ecuador in 1994. It continued by my side when we decided to focus on repeat medical trips to Tricotte, a small village in the northwestern part of the country where between 1997 and 2002 we returned five times.

Each trip had its own unusual challenges, but we always sensed God's presence with us in strong and powerful ways. However, one of the biggest challenges came on our trip in March 1997. Marken, a seventeen-year-old, lived two hours walking distance away from us. He and his mom came to see me because of a tennis ball-size tumor at the back of his neck. It had been slowly growing for several years. Marken was made fun of by his peers and he'd threatened to try and cut it off himself with a machete. Then one day he heard there was a medical team from the US in Tricotte.

Initially I was uncertain that I could take this tumor off for fear of deeper attached structures and potentially serious bleeding. However, as I examined him more closely it didn't seem to be attached to anything except the skin. So after praying for wisdom and skill I, and Physician Assistant, Randy Mancuso, another team member, decided to try and remove it. Amazingly it came off much easier than I'd expected and the patient was so happy and grateful. I took the tumor to a pathologist friend at Methodist

Hospital. He found it to be a basal cell skin cancer, very rare in a young man.

On our next trip two years later, Marken returned for a follow-up visit. There was excellent healing with only a small surgical scar and no recurrence. Marken's life had been forever changed.

Because of certain conditions that developed in some towns along the road to Tricotte following our last trip, Dio, our Haitian pastor, didn't feel it was safe for us to go back. That ended mission trips for me and my bag. I've always felt sadness over never being able to return to Tricotte because of the safety issue. My team members and I were thankful for the time spent there, touching many lives on behalf of our Great Physician, yet regretful that we couldn't come back.

After I shared this with Steve he told me more about Bruno Exame who was to get my bag. At the time, Bruno would have been somewhere between nine to fifteen. Steve recalled how Bruno had followed him wherever he went during those trips. I'd probably examined his parents and even Bruno himself, no doubt examining his ears with my otoscope. Bruno is now twenty-six, married, with one small child, born and raised in Tricotte, the village where Pastor Dio was also born and raised.

So sometime during this ten-day mission trip with a youth group from Church of the Open Door, Steve and Pastor Dio will meet with Bruno, and probably his family, to give him my doctor's bag. I know Dio will be very excited and grateful, as I'm sure Bruno will be also. I'm deeply honored and privileged to give Bruno my bag, which I feel is more than just a bag being given to him.

When my son Matt heard this story he said, "It's like a mantle being passed on."

I feel like I have a new son, certainly a brother in Christ, a physician friend who longs to bring hope and healing to his people. As I let those thoughts into my spirit I wept deeply for a minute or so, filled with joy and gratitude that I had a small part in helping a young physician start his journey of ministering to others. I now pray for and have a strong yearning that some day Anna and I will return to Haiti to meet Bruno and his family as I desire to prayer-fully impart more of myself into him.

Though this brings me to the end of the chapters in this book, it's not the end of my journey. I believe, by faith, that God wants us to complete all our grandparenting trips, which will take another seven years. I know that He still has many other "good works" for each of us to do. Fortunately, longevity is on both our sides.

But there will come a day when each of us will be called home as stated in Psalm 84:7 (NIV), *They go from strength to strength till each appears before God in Zion.* Oh what a glorious homecoming that will be! I look forward to that day with great anticipation.

EPILOGUE

I write this primarily for my dear, dear, grandchildren and the future generations. However, all readers of this book are invited to" listen in" and receive from the Holy Spirit whatever He may have for you.

When God created you, He included a sanctified imagination. I'm asking now that you use this gift to imagine that you and I are together, sitting on chairs facing each other, toe-to-toe, knee-to-knee, and looking each other in the eyes. We're both relaxed, smiling, and enjoying being together. Time is nonexistent in this setting.

My desire is to end this book by sharing my seven heart-cries for you. It's not only my wish, but your Nona's as well. We've been asking our heavenly Father these requests since your mom and dad first knew you were present and growing in your mom's womb. We will keep on interceding for you, with hearts of gratitude, as long as we live. And we're asking that He will answer these prayers in your life in the name of His Son, Jesus, and by the power of the Holy Spirit.

1) God's Great Love For You

My first desire for you is that you will come to know and experience how much God truly loves you. **You are the apple of His eye.** He loves you unconditionally. Nothing you can say or do will ever separate you from His love. This is beautifully stated in Romans 8:38–39 (NASB) where the apostle Paul says: *"For I am* *convinced that neither death, nor life, nor angels, nor principalities, nor things present, nor things to come, nor powers, nor height, nor depth, nor any other created thing, shall be able to separate us from the love of God, which is in Christ Jesus our Lord."*

My prayer is that you will let this truth into your spirit, soul, and body. As you grow in your understanding and embrace His great love for you, your life will be transformed and you will grow in your intimacy and love for Him. I pray this will lead you into a hunger and thirst for Him as portrayed by the psalmist when he cried out to God in Psalm 63:1 (KJV), *"O God, Thou art my God; I shall seek Thee earnestly; My soul thirsts for Thee, my flesh yearns for Thee, in a dry and weary land where there is no water."*

At this point, I want to tell you how this has played out in my life. I've shared much of my story in chapter ten but this is a significant addition. I shared with you how I'd had a totally wrong view of God as well as a wrong view of myself. I thought that emotionally I was an introvert, only comfortable around very good friends. I was quite adept at covering up my inner feelings so that I looked good on the outside, but inside I was very anxious and fearful around people.

After I started attending Miracles in the Market Place, as shared earlier, I put a name to my inner struggle. I had a "fear of people" because of the distorted view of myself, a phrase I'd heard from Pastors Craig Nelson and Vivian Klebs. They repeatedly challenged me to get out of my comfort zone and reach out in love to people. The key verse that impacted me deeply was, and still is, 1 John 4:18 (NIV), *"There is no fear in love. But perfect love drives out fear, because fear has to do with punishment. The one who fears is not made perfect in love."*

I began praying for divine appointments where the Spirit would lead me to talk to someone at McDonald's, Rainbow grocery store, servers at our restaurant table or someone who came to our home to do repair work we had ordered. I was scared to death to begin with because it was so "not me" to approach a stranger and ask if there was anything over which I could pray for them, or simply tell them how much God loved them. But I continually asked the Holy Spirit to empower me to love that person and to see him or her as my heavenly Father does.

One thing that helped me push through my fear, besides the above verse, was something in one of Pastor Vivian's messages. She said, "Remember you have the Father, the Son, and the Holy Spirit in you, around you, and beside you. There's no greater powerhouse to have with you, so go for it—whatever you are being led to do or say."

As a result I've had many amazing encounters that have brought encouragement and hope to others and great joy to my own soul.

This growth in me hasn't been easy because there have been times when fear has raised its ugly head. For example, in the fall of 2013 I received a phone call from an old friend from a previous church we'd attended, who had organized a monthly breakfast for men in that church to get together for fellowship and to renew our connectedness with each other. I agreed to come, but inwardly the old fear and anxiety resurfaced. I began thinking about what I would say and worried about what they would think of me. I went a couple of times but felt very uncomfortable and full of fear. I was real good at covering up my feelings so I'd look good on the outside. Inside, however, I knew it was my old false self rising to the surface. And I began to consider no longer attending.

It was during this time that Anna and I flew out to California to visit our two sons, Dan and Matt, and their respective families. We were with Matt and Tami and their kiddos when I began to journal my feelings of not returning to this men's breakfast group. The Spirit soon opened my eyes that I had hooked into feelings I'd had thirty-five years prior, which were just as fresh as they'd been then. He also showed me why I had them. I wrote, *"You don't love them! You are focusing on your feelings and not seeing them as God sees them."* When I realized that, I dropped to my knees in tears, went to the cross, and confessed my sin of self-centeredness, knowing I was only looking at myself and my own insecurities.

That evening I shared my struggle and insight with Matt and Tami. In their Spirit-led wisdom, they saw my struggle as a curse perpetrated by Satan himself, coming down from previous generations. It was the evil one who had tricked me into this negative thinking about myself. They prayed over me, breaking that generational curse, commanding Satan to get out of my life, and asking the Spirit to fill me with the Father's love for people, especially the men in the breakfast group.

I felt like a weight had been lifted from my shoulders. In my imagination I could see a long cord extending from me and going back several generations, which now was lying on the ground, totally severed from my body. I was set free!

I've been to many breakfast meetings with those men since and it has been a joy. All fear and anxiety is totally gone and I look forward to each meeting with anticipation. I see each man as an incredible creation of God and I feel so blessed to be a part of that group.

A few months ago I experienced something else that also deeply impacted me. I'd read somewhere that someone who fears others won't be able to look people in the eyes as they talk with them. I realized that had been true with me, and to some extent, still existed. So I began asking the Holy Spirit to empower me to look people in the eye.

I volunteered to serve communion at our church the next time there was an opportunity. I prayed all week for God's love to flow through me and for His Spirit to enable me to truly see the people as I served them. On Saturday, as I prepared for Sunday, an interesting thing happened.

I needed something from the Rainbow grocery store near our home. As I was driving there, I asked God to give me a divine appointment. I could sense in my spirit that He had someone for me to meet. As I approached the entrance, I noticed an elderly couple heading for the same door but coming from a different direction. They walked slowly as the lady was limping. I sensed the Spirit's nudge to speak with them.

Once inside the store I approached them, introduced myself, and asked if I could pray for healing from whatever was hurting her leg. They were surprised but quickly said they'd be glad for me to pray. We talked about her condition for a bit, then I prayed that Jesus would bring His healing. To which they were deeply blessed and grateful. Although I didn't see any immediate signs of healing, I felt great joy that His presence was very strong and had touched all three of us. It may have been a "HIP" (healing in progress) experience, but I left it all in His hands and knew the couple felt the Father's love for them.

The next morning, I was informed that I would be serving alone at my communion station because of a shortage of servers, which was okay with me. I experienced a real freedom looking people in the eye as I served them. I sensed His Presence and was filled with incredible joy as I gave the elements to those who came my way.

After the service, I felt drawn to spend time at the cross by the altar. I first knelt, then prostrated myself. His presence was strong. It was so precious to simply be there with my Abba. As I lay there, I sensed in my spirit that He was speaking to me. I didn't hear any audible words but what I felt He said was, *"This is how I created you. This is your true self beginning to blossom as I intended. I'm so glad you're seeing yourself as I've seen you all along, before the foundation of the world."* I realized this was now my "new normal." I wept for joy and gratefulness as I basked in my Abba's love and His rejoicing over me. I felt like the "great cloud of witnesses," referred to in Hebrews 12:1, were standing up cheering for me.

In no way do I want to imply that I feel I've "arrived." I know I'm a long ways off, but I have a hunger and thirst for more of Him that I pray will never cease. This has been a mountaintop experience I'll never forget. However, I yearn to have the same attitude the apostle Paul writes about in Philippians 3:12 (NASB), *"Not that I have already obtained it, or have already become perfect, but I press on in order that I may lay hold of that for which also I was laid hold of by Christ Jesus."*

Now, my dear one, my heart's cry for you is that you will seek hard after God. This is far more than Sunday morning church or saying, "Hi" to Him occasionally during the week, which is what I did many years of my life. It's realizing the love and goodness of God toward you in first, creating you, and then desiring an intimate relationship with you, which draws you to Him. But your heavenly Father is a real "gentleman" who never forces Himself on you. He loves you so much He *waits* for you to move toward Him.

David said it this way in Psalm 27:8 (NIV), *"My heart says of you, ' Seek his face!' Your face, LORD, I will seek."*

Jeremiah 29:13–14a (NASB, emphasis mine) records what God said to those in exile in Babylon, " *'You will seek Me and find Me when you search for Me with all your heart. I will be found by you,' declares the LORD."* So as you pursue Him and "find" Him you will be overwhelmed with His great love for you as well as for all His creation. This leads me to the next prayer I have for you.

2) Learn to Love Yourself

As you receive His love flowing in you, your eyes will be opened to the importance of loving yourself. Jesus made this clear in an encounter he had with one of the teachers of the law who asked Him in Mark 12:28b–31 (NIV, emphasis mine), " *'Of all the commandments, which is the most important?' 'The most important one,' answered Jesus, 'is this: "Hear, O Israel: The Lord our God, the Lord is one. Love the Lord your God with all your heart and with all your soul and with all your mind and with all your strength." The second is this: "Love your neighbor* **as yourself***." There is no commandment greater then these.' "*

Note that this is a command, not just a good idea or wishful thinking. I've lived most of my life not liking myself, although I never realized it at the time.

In 1989, your Nona and I were blessed to attend a conference taught by Jeff Van Vondern, a counseling pastor at Church of the Open Door. The title of the conference was: "Wounded by Shame, Healed by Grace." His opening teaching was that each of us have three basic needs: 1) I am loved and accepted—unconditionally, which is not based on any certain behavior; 2) I am worthwhile and capable, which is not based on performance; and, 3) I am not alone.

I'm asking you to pause, reflect on what I wrote, and let it in. And I have a challenge for you. I'm very serious about this and trust that you will do this. Every morning when you get up, or sometime during your day, look at yourself in a mirror and say out loud: 1) "Today, I know I am loved and accepted. I choose to love myself; 2) I am worthwhile and capable; and, 3) I am not alone."

This may be a hard thing for you to do at first. It certainly was for me. You may even think, "I'm nutso" or "I've lost it," but that's simply the evil one giving you those thoughts. He doesn't want you seeing yourself as God sees you. Instead he wants you thinking, "I'm no good," "I don't measure up," or other negative thoughts you may have. At this point you need to say out loud and *with authority*: "In the strong name of Jesus, get the heck out of here, Satan. I'm going to say what is true about myself." As you do that it will be the best "self-care" you can ever give yourself.

I have another challenge for you. Memorize 1 Corinthians 13, the love chapter. Bathe your spirit, soul, and mind in that passage. Ask your heavenly Father, in the strong name of Jesus and by the power the Holy Spirit, to empower you to become that to yourself as well as to others.

I close this longing for you with a prayer that Paul expressed to the church at Ephesus. Ephesians 3:16–19 (NIV), *"I pray that out of his glorious riches he may strengthen you with power through his Spirit in your inner being, so that Christ may dwell in your hearts through faith. And I pray that you, being rooted and established in love, 'may have power, together with all the Lord's holy people, to grasp how wide and long and high and deep is the love of Christ, and to know this love that surpasses knowledge—that you may be filled to the measure of all the fullness of God.' "*

3) Discover Your Passion(s)

I want to introduce my next heart's cry for you with a question. What passion(s) did your Creator have in mind as He thought about you from before the foundation of the world? Ephesians 1:4–6 (MSG) says, *"Long before he laid down earth's foundations, he had us in mind, had settled on us as a focus of his love, to be made whole and holy by his love. Long, long ago he decided to adopt us into his family through Jesus Christ. (What pleasure he took in planning this!) He wanted us to enter into the celebration of his lavish gift-giving by the hand of his beloved Son."*

Now I want you to imagine that before you were conceived, you were sitting down with God, who hands you an envelope. *"In here,"* He explains, *"are the sealed orders for your life."* (The passion He has put within the core of your being.) He wants you to know and to pursue what He has created in you.

In a sense, He has concealed the passion He created in you so that you may uncover and embrace it. Proverbs 25:2 (MSG) says, *"God delights in concealing things; scientists delight in discovering things."* There will be nothing more exciting and satisfying for you than to discover what He has lovingly put within you. You'll find it life-giving because you will enjoy doing what He has created you to do.

In 1999, I was given a small book as a gift, titled *Healing the Purpose of Your Life.* There I was introduced to the term "sealed orders." The authors defined this as "our special way of being." As

I read through the book and did the exercises they suggested, I felt they were talking about the purpose and passion of my life. I prayerfully thought about that for a period of time until it became clear that my purpose was not a profession, position, or job, but was contained in the phrase, "Compassion to see wholeness restored." As I look at my life, to His glory, that's what I now see.

This was certainly the underlying reason I felt God's leading me to be a family physician. Though the profession had its challenges, I never once wanted to do something else. The privilege of doing medical mission work in many different countries on a short-term basis grew out of my passion. It also was the underlying reason for many of the ministries I've been involved in, especially the prayer ministry that Nona and I have been privileged to be a part of at our church the past fifteen years.

Many people go through life without truly knowing the purpose for which God created them. I know that won't happen to you as you prayerfully pursue Him and ask the Holy Spirit to reveal this to you. I'm excited for you to learn and pursue the passion that is in you.

4) Learn to Listen for God's Voice

The fourth desire and prayer I have is for you to understand and practice what I call, "correct spiritual alignment," which I'll explain. We're impacted in many ways by our culture with all its rapidly developing technology, pressure to succeed, and demands to go faster. This often leaves us breathless, frustrated, and out of sorts with ourselves and others, with the emphasis on the use of our brains to figure things out and to plan our days.

I believe, and suggest to you, that this is a misalignment of our total being. To use a common expression, "we get the cart before the horse" when we use our brain to lead the way. Paul says what I believe is the right alignment in 1 Thessalonians 5:23 (NASB), *"Now may the God of peace sanctify you entirely; and may your spirit and soul and body be preserved complete, without blame at the coming of our Lord Jesus Christ."*

It's our spirit that should lead us, as led by the Holy Spirit, followed by our soul (mind, will, emotion) and then our body. Our mind is so important but must be led by our spirit.

Most of my life I've tried to figure things out with my head, not realizing that my spirit was to be the leader. Let me give you a personal illustration that happened early in the writing of this book.

It was a little less than a year ago when I sat down to write one day. "Holy Spirit, dictate to me," I prayed before I started that day as usual, but instead of being quiet and listening for Him to speak to me, I immediately thought, "What should I write next?" My brain was in full gear trying to figure out what I would say next to say to my grandkids. This went on for thirty or forty minutes and I was getting nowhere. Then it dawned on me (I believe it was the Holy Spirit nudging me), I was out of alignment. I should be asking the Holy Spirit, "What do my grandkids need to hear from me?" Then I had to listen with my spirit to hear what He brought to my mind. Once I made that shift there was a remarkable change and the words began to flow. The key is learning to *listen* to the Holy Spirit.

I believe the triune Godhead is speaking to us all the time. Psalm 139:17–18a (NASB) says, *"How precious also are Your thoughts to me, O God! How vast is the sum of them! If I should count them, they would outnumber the sand."* Since God is thinking about us all the time, then surely He is talking to us as well.

David also tells us how much God's creation speaks to us in Psalm 19:1–2 (NIV), *"The heavens declare the glory of God; the skies proclaim the work of his hands. Day after day they pour forth speech; night after night they reveal knowledge."*

Learning to listen to the Holy Spirit is a spiritual discipline that I hadn't realized most of my life. I highly recommend a book that helped me a great deal, *Invitation to Solitude and Silence,* by Ruth Haley Barton. The author takes you by the hand, so to speak, and helps you become quiet, sit in His presence, and learn to listen.

Another book I recommend is *Getting to Know the Holy Spirit,* by Mahesh and Bonnie Chavda. This will give you further understanding of the Holy Spirit's work in your life.

Make listening to the Spirit a frequent exercise throughout your day. For years I had a quiet time in the morning, then took off for the day without thinking of God's presence going with me. Now I pause frequently so I can be quiet, listen to, and talk with Him. I still need and yearn to grow in this area of my life.

In John 14:16–17, 26b (NASB), Jesus made it clear to His disciples and to us of the role of the Holy Spirit. *"I will ask the Father, and He will give you another Helper, that He may be with you forever; that is the Spirit of truth, whom the world cannot receive, because it does not behold Him or know Him, but you know Him because He abides with you, and will be in you. . . . He will teach you all things, and bring to your remembrance all that I said to you."*

5) Welcome Interruptions

This leads me to the fifth challenge I have for you, which is very practical and can transform negative emotions of frustration and anger into joy. Think about it, is that something that you would like to experience?

In chapter thirteen, I introduced this to you out of my own experience. But now I want to ask you a couple of questions. First, what is one of the most common things that can happen to you that brings frustration and anger almost immediately to the surface? It can be a little thing, something major, or anything in between. I'm quite sure for most people it's one word: interruptions. On any given day unexpected things happen that you didn't plan.

Second, why do interruptions in our schedule bring about such negative emotions in us? It's because we want to be in control of our day, and interruptions mean that something beyond us has taken over. I confess that most of my life I've been a "control freak," getting upset over anything imaginable, especially finances, which is why I wrote chapter thirteen.

So I'd like to suggest three steps to change a negative emotion following an interruption, into a positive one—from frustration to joy.

1. Own up to the truth that you have a control issue. Call it what it is. Share your struggle with another safe and reliable person(s). Bring it to the cross and request forgiveness and cleansing. Ask the Holy Spirit to empower you to change, because you cannot change yourself.

2. Make it a daily practice when you get out of bed each morning to give the day to God. He is the one who created that day for you. Psalm 118:24 (NASB) says, *"This is the day which the LORD has made; let us rejoice and be glad in it."* As you do that, ask Him to empower you to welcome any interruptions that come your way.

3. When an interruption comes, pause and remind yourself, "God is in control of this day—not me." He loves to make "all things work together for good," so choose to rejoice and thank Him that He will cause good to come out of this event.

This is not easy to do but like anything else it takes discipline and persistence with your attention focused, not on yourself, whether you fail or succeed, but on Him. He is the one, by the power of the Holy Spirit, who brings transformation.

This is where trust triumphs over control. Scripture is full of encouragement for us to trust, rest, and wait. I've never found a verse that says to "try harder to control." In fact, if you look deeper at what is behind control, besides your own pride, you'll find the evil one whispering negative thoughts into your ear/mind.

Some of my favorite verses that help me when I face an interruption are: Romans 8:28 (NASB, emphasis mine), *"And we know that God causes* all *things to work together for good to those who love God, to those who are called according to His purpose."*

Deuteronomy 33:12b (NIV), *"Let the beloved of the* LORD *rest secure in Him, for He shields him all day long, and the one the* LORD *loves rests between his shoulders."* And

Proverbs 16:9 (NASB), *"The mind of man plans his way, but the* LORD *directs his steps."*

6) Treasuring God's Word

My next prayer for you is found in Psalm 119:9–11 (NASB, emphasis mine): *"How can a young man keep his way pure? By keeping it according to Your word. With all my heart I have sought you; do not let me wander from Your commandments. Your word I have* treasured *in my heart, that I may not sin against You."*

I pray that you will learn the discipline of memorizing and meditating on key Scripture passages. His Word is His "love letters" to you personally. He yearns for you to treasure them in your heart, like a most precious gem, and to think about them as you go through your day.

Your mind is often a battlefield against negative thoughts, as I've mentioned previously. Satan is behind every negative thought you've ever had. So you need a key verse hidden in your heart to take those thoughts captive, as Paul writes in 2 Corinthians 10:3–5 (NASB), *"For though we walk in the flesh, we do not war according to the flesh, for the weapons of our warfare are not of the flesh, but divinely powerful for the destruction of fortresses. We are destroying speculations and every lofty thing raised up against the knowledge of God, and are taking every thought captive to the obedience of Christ."*

I'll give you an example of how this worked in my life. Early one Monday morning a couple of years ago, I was up and feeling well, with no symptoms of any health problems. Suddenly I had the urge to cough and up came a significant amount of blood, which happened again five minutes later. I had no chest pain, shortness of breath, or any other symptoms so I said to myself, "This isn't good!"

As a family doc, I could easily think of several possibilities, none of them very good. I began to experience significant anxiety, and fear rose up within me. I prayed but still remained emotionally shaken up. This went on for thirty minutes or so. Then a familiar Scripture verse came to my mind, which I know was prompted by the Holy Spirit. I'd quoted it to myself many times when feeling anxious or fearful. It was Philippians 4:4–7 (NASB), *"Rejoice in the Lord always and again I will say, rejoice. Let your gentle spirit be known to all men. The Lord is near. Be anxious for nothing, but in everything by prayer and supplication with thanksgiving let your requests be made known to God. And the peace of God, which surpasses all comprehension, will guard your hearts and your minds in Christ Jesus."*

I quoted those verses several times, then said out loud, "I choose to rejoice! I know, Abba, You didn't cause this, but I know that You are with me in whatever this turns out to be. I also know that You cause all things to work together for good." An amazing thing happened, the anxiety and fear totally dissipated in an instant. In its place I felt joy, peace, and a wonderful sense of His presence. It was like I'd turned off the switch of darkness and turned on the switch of His light. I shifted from looking at myself and my fears to focusing on my Abba and His goodness. This peace has never left.

I was able to get an appointment with a doctor later in the morning. That set off a series of tests and scans ending up with a diagnosis of a very small pulmonary infarction. A small blood clot had broken loose somewhere in my legs or pelvis and traveled to my right lung. I'm on a blood-thinner to prevent that from happening again.

It's my desire that you will learn to treasure key passages in your heart. They will become a reservoir of living water that the Spirit will remind you of at the right time and place.

7) Trust and Obey

This brings me to my last, but not least, heart's cry for you, which is that you remember the most often repeated promise in Scripture—a five-word statement God spoke to Israel repeatedly as well as to individuals. He speaks the same to us: "I will be with you."

I like the way King David says from his perspective in Psalm 23:4a (NKJV, emphasis mine), *"Yea, though I walk through the valley of the shadow of death, I will fear no evil; for You are with me."*

Our problem can be, as it was for Israel, that we forget the promise or choose to ignore it because we think we can do better ourselves. In this business of life we forget to pause and remember that He is with us. I've done that so many times over the years and it's made life very difficult. Whenever I tried to do something in my own strength, it never panned out well.

In your life you've already gone through struggles and there will be plenty more. That's life! God not only gives you the promise of His presence but He asks you the question, *"Can you trust Me?"* That's where the rubber really meets the road, so to speak.

I have no doubt that you see God as one who is trustworthy, who created you, who loves you, and has a wonderful plan for your life. But this is where faith comes in, as Paul said in *2* Corinthians 5:7 (NASB), *"For we walk by faith, not by sight."* The challenge is to take your eyes off of your difficult situations and focus on Him instead. As you trust Him you will experience peace and joy beyond your expectations.

I love the verses, Isaiah 26: 3–4 (NASB, emphasis mine), *"The* *steadfast of mind You will keep in perfect peace, because he trusts in You. Trust in the L*ORD *forever, for in God the L*ORD*, we have an everlasting Rock."*

I would like to share with you how this has played out in your Nona's and my life this past year. As you know, we've loved our lake home on Medicine Lake. As of the last of June 2014, we'd been privileged to live there for twenty-four years. We thought and dreamed that we would stay there forever, or at least for a lot more years.

As mentioned earlier, we had a major wake-up call in the second week of June. Nona, who handles our finances, told me that we were going into the red. Her statement, "We can't continue to live on the lake" hit us like a ton of bricks! We had increasing expenses from health issues and property taxes. When we combined that with the increasing awareness that we no longer had the physical strength to maintain our lake home, we had no alternative. We had to downsize and sell our home.

As we talked and prayed about our situation, we knew God was in this with us. He was not abandoning us, but He did ask, *"Can you trust me?"* We knew He was totally trustworthy and that we could and would trust Him. But we had no idea how He would orchestrate all the things that would have to fall into place. And you know something? We didn't have to know, that was His business. It was amazing how He put things together we could never have anticipated.

We had planned for months to try and have a family reunion at our home the last week of July, for whoever could come. It didn't look like many of our kids and grandkids would make it. After announcing our plans, the reunion switched to, "How can we help Papa and Nona to downsize and get the house ready for sale?" More family came than we'd expected.

As we continued working on the house, we began diligently looking for an apartment to rent. We wanted a three-bedroom so we could have a guest room and an office. We also wanted a washer and dryer in our unit, along with an underground garage. As we searched, we found an apartment with those criteria were few and far between in the Plymouth-Maple Grove area, especially having a vacancy in the fall. We kept praying and trusting.

Early on in our search beginning in August, I'd found that Hummingbird Cove in Plymouth met our criteria and was available the first part of September. However, we kept looking until August came to an end. We were getting tired of searching, so we decided to take a second look on the third of September. It was difficult to get a good picture of the apartment because three families were then living in it, with shoes and clothes all over the place. We told the manager that we had no prospective buyer for our house at that time, so had no idea when we might move in.

For some reason, we must have found favor with her because she said she would hold it for two months until November 1. We had to pay the application fee and security deposit amounting to $480. We talked it over with our realtors and financial advisor who thought it was worth the risk, since we were quite confident our house would sell. We were very relieved and grateful to have the apartment question settled.

We wanted to sell our pontoon but, Joe Harty, who took care of winterizing it, said, "It will have to sell before the end of September because no one buys pontoons in October." So we advertised on his website and Nona put it on Craig's List. We had a lot of people respond, even some who wanted to take a second look yet never showed up.

We'll never forget that Thursday, September 25. The pontoon had been on Craig's List for two weeks and, therefore, was buried at the bottom of the advertisement list. Nona was trying to figure out how she could raise it to the top and called our daughter-in-law Tami in California, since she was a whiz at working Craig's List, but neither had any success.

Nona was feeling sorry about taking so much of Tami's time

and was going to suggest they stop trying, when Tami shouted, "It just came to the top! I don't know what happened but there it is." Half an hour or so later the phone rang and it was a gentleman who'd just seen the pontoon ad and wanted to come over with his wife to check it out. He'd been looking off and on for weeks and it turned out to be just what he was hoping for. So he bought our pontoon. That sale gave us greater confidence that the house would also sell in God's timing.

A couple had looked at our house in the middle of September but made no offer. Since our first Open House on August 10 we'd had many lookers but no offers. However, this one couple watched and waited and then made an offer when they felt the price was right. There was a little negotiating but ultimately we agreed. That was on October 12. Oh how we rejoiced!

Before we had any idea when the house would sell, we'd been thinking about an estate sale afterward, but didn't know who to turn to. Nona was in our bank one day to cash in some old coins we'd found in my dad's box of stuff. The bank teller thought some of the coins were worth a lot more than she could pay her. In the course of their conversation, Nona mentioned our desire to find someone to hold an estate sale for us. The teller mentioned that there was a gentleman in that business who regularly came to the bank for his Monday morning deposit of his past weekend earnings. She offered to give him Nona's name and phone number. That put us in touch with the perfect one to do the sale.

We met with him early in September to make some tentative plans based on his schedule and when our house sold. We were glad to learn that after the sale anything left of value would go to charity and everything else remaining to "1-800-Got-Junk." Following that he'd arrange to have the house thoroughly cleaned and ready for the new owners. That was a real relief for us.

There are so many other ways God orchestrated events in our behalf but I'll share only one more. The cost of getting the house ready for sale was not in our budget at the start of the year. Consequently things became financially tight.

One day near the end of September, Nona got a call from our banker. An anonymous individual had put a thousand dollars in our checking account. We have no idea who it was but we were very grateful for the timely gift.

The journey we'd been on, trusting and waiting to see how God was going to work this difficult situation for His glory and our good, has been an incredible experience for us. We have grown a great deal in learning to trust and obey.

Not always does a difficult situation turn out as positively as we've experienced. Many times the result is not what we initially wanted. However, God knows what is best for us and He is with us in every situation. We know that all things do work together for our good when He is in charge.

In closing, I want to say again how precious you are to your Nona and me. Life, for us, has become so much richer, fuller, and exciting because of you. Like on our grandparenting trip, you got us to do things we never dreamed about doing ourselves. You have enriched our lives in ways you may never realize, but we do.

We are so grateful for God's gift to us of you. That's why our heart's cry is for you to pursue God with your whole heart, to love yourself, and to be His vessel of love to others.

We have had a wonderful life and still do. We desire the same for you, and you will have it as you keep your eyes focused on Him. God's best to you!

Love,
Papa and Nona

Acknowledgments

It is a delight to recall over the last four years all those who helped and encouraged me along the way in writing my book. I'm deeply grateful.

The first one I want to thank and give praise to is God himself for the three things he gave me. First, He created me with the gift of writing that I didn't fully realize I had until six years ago. Secondly, He gave me a desire to write and leave a legacy for my grandkids, which grew into a deep, burning passion within my soul. The third and most amazing thing He did was to partner with me in my writing. Every time I sat down with pencil in hand I was aware of His presence. That was a new experience for me.

I am deeply appreciative of David Sluka who has been like a mentor to me through his book, *Write Your Book*. I first met David in the spring of 2012. I learned that he was a writer, speaker, author, and coach. I attended one of his writer's workshops that gave me a good start. Later, when his book came out in 2014, I had the step-by-step guide I needed to write my manuscript. When that was completed I turned it over to him and Hit the Mark Publishing, which brought my book through to completion.

The next person I owe kudos to is my dear wife, Anna. She never doubted I could write even though early on I wasn't so sure myself. She has been my first editor all along the way. A misspelled word never was missed. Her repeated statements about something I had just written such as, "excellent" or "that is really good," truly encouraged me.

I felt like I had a small "cloud of witnesses surrounding me" cheering me on in my family. They were Dan and Rose, Debbie and Dave, Becky and Dan, Melanie and Craig, Matt and Tami, my brother Bill and his wife Shirley, and my sister Jeannie and her husband Verne. Frequently, when I sent a part of my writing to my kids, I would get back, "That's awesome, Dad. Keep it up."

I want to highlight four of my family members in their encouragement of me.

1) Tami, my daughter-in-law, was relentless early on in stating, "You have a book in you. You have to get it out." That started around 2008 after I had started writing short stories of my life. Anna, jokingly said, "She really is bugging you." My only response was, "Yeah, she sure is." I'm grateful that she saw in me what I didn't see at that time.

2) When I was early on in my writing, (August 2012), Matt sent me a very meaningful prayer which I repeated each time I sat down to write. "God I pray for a cocoon of protection around Dad as he writes so that distractions will be kept at bay. I pray for his mind to be focused and for a flow of thoughts from his spirit that is inspired by you. Bless him with joy as he experiences your presence through writing, God. Amen"

3) Becky offered me a deeply appreciated suggestion when we were visiting her and her family in Florida during April, 2015. She lovingly but firmly recommended that I replace my goal to complete my manuscript from, "sometime in the fall" to a date-specific target. I realized she was right and the next day I announced my writing will be complete on September 13, my birthday. Everyone cheered. Amazingly, God orchestrated time

and events over the summer to allow me to finish my manuscript precisely on that day.

4) Melanie gave me, what I felt was a brilliant idea, when we visited her and her family in Iowa the third week of May. I was struggling with trying to dictate what I had written on paper into my computer. I shared that with her, and she offered a two-part solution: "Buy a Dictaphone and hire a typist. Let her do what you don't do very well. Stick to writing, which you do well." The result was a big turnaround in my writing production.

I am very thankful to Wanda for becoming my typist. She did a marvelous job for me and gave hope that I could complete my writing on schedule. I had a double bonus from her since she also did a great job editing my book.

A wonderful gift came to me when I joined the Open Door Church writer's group a year and half ago. It was a rich and helpful experience to learn from other writers. (The special snacks added to the evening and made great munchies). Also there was a special community-like blessing when we shared prayer requests and lifted each other up before the LORD. I'm so appreciative for this meaningful group: Stacy, Karen, Amber, Autumn, Becky, Bill, Colleen, Dan, Sandy, Scott, Jennifer, Doug, Eric, Jeff, Karen, Mari, Mary, Nina, Robert, Stephen, Thomas, Tim, and Vanessa.

There were many other family and friends who encouraged me and expressed excitement by saying, "I can't wait to read your book." Thanks to all of you. You are very special to me.

Made in the USA
Lexington, KY
26 July 2017